Preflight Checklist

Is Self-Employment for You?

Preflight Checklist

Is Self-Employment for You?
Second Edition

Paul E. Casey

ISBN-13: 978-1542382878
ISBN-10: 1542382874

This book is dedicated to my wife Marti, my chosen partner, and to our two (mostly) delightful canine "assistants," Puff and Sadie Mae. I also dedicate it to my family and practically everyone else I have crossed paths with during this incredible journey through life.

TABLE OF CONTENTS

....

Preflight Checklist

INTRODUCTION

I don't know about you, but before I listen to the advice of others, I want to know what gives them the credentials to share their wisdom with me. For example, if I'm flying somewhere, I'm more inclined to listen to a pilot's advice on how to deal with air turbulence than a passenger's. If I'm watching TV and someone in a white coat tells me I should take a certain drug in order to treat something, I find myself wondering if he or she is really a doctor.

Right now, you're probably wondering: Who is this fellow, Paul E. Casey? And what gives him the credentials to write this book?

Well, I'll tell you. I'm a self-employed business owner who has run a successful communications business for over twenty-five years. I'm also the former host of several radio talk shows about self-employment, in which I've talked to hundreds of successful entrepreneurs about their experiences. I've learned that, while there's no one way to guarantee success, there are some basic fundamentals that successful entrepreneurs get right. In this book, I'll share what I've learned about self-employment with you.

I've heard that 80 percent of small businesses fail. I believe the major reason why so many entrepreneurs fail is because they are inundated with bad advice. My mission in this book is not to try to talk you into going into business for yourself. It's to put you in the strongest possible position to make that determination for yourself, and to do so with facts, not fantasy. Always remember this: Anyone can start a business but only a few can sustain a business.

Faster than a speeding bullet

Twitter, YouTube, smartphones, Wi-Fi; touch screens, bionic limbs, hybrid cars, flying drones that are making package deliveries. What do all these things have in common? When I wrote the first edition of *Is Self-Employment for You?* back in 2003, all the inventions listed above didn't even exist. Or if they did exist, they weren't yet on the consumer market or in general widespread use.

So much has changed in the last ten to twelve years. But that's not surprising. We've been going through an unstoppable high-tech revolution for the past forty years. New technologies are introduced every day. We buy them, we use them, and just a few years or months later, they're considered outdated.

The smartphones, computers, servers, networks, game consoles, and handheld devices that we use today are smaller, faster, cheaper, and perform better than those we used ten years ago. The websites on the Internet are faster, more colorful, and more interactive. They give you more content, more video, and more social interaction.

The TV sets are larger and relatively less expensive. But they give you better digital pictures and far more entertainment options. Depending on your broadband provider, you might even be able to access the Internet on your HDTV, something unheard of ten years ago.

In 1986, just before I started my own business, I attended a charity event where a cell phone the size of a shoe was auctioned off for $1,500. Today, that cell phone model is in a museum somewhere. Now you can get a smartphone for free. It fits right in your pocket, accesses the Web, takes photos and movies, sends text messages to your friends, etc.

In the 1990s, desktop publishing software allowed me to greatly reduce the cost of designing and publishing my own newspaper. Today, publishing is almost free! Everyone publishes online "blogs," or sends out eNewsletters. And you're reading this second edition of my book as a Kindle book, a format that didn't even exist when I wrote the first edition.

So when I went back and re-read my original book, I didn't know what to expect. As I read it, I asked myself,

"What's different about opening a business today, as compared to ten years ago? If I wrote the book today, would it tell a dramatically different story? Would all the high-tech advancements we've had in the past ten years make a difference in the success or failure of a self-employed entrepreneur?"

The short answer is no.

The fact is, most of what I wrote in the original book is still valid today. With all the new technologies, *the basic principles for starting and sustaining a successful business remain the same.* If you're a self-employed business owner, your success or failure will not be based on technology, but on the effort you put into your business and the decisions you make.

All the high-tech tools we have now make it easier to *conduct* business. Your website is basically an online marketing brochure, allowing your potential clients to learn more about your business. If it's an eCommerce site, it gives them an easy way to buy your product online. Your blog and Twitter accounts make it easy to post your opinions for others to read. LinkedIn makes it easier to find the right contact person at a company you'd like to have as a client. Google and Facebook allow you to create online ads and mobile marketing campaigns. Email and eNewsletters make it easy to keep in touch with your clients, and email marketing makes it easy to send out special offers and daily deals.

But it's still up to you to *build* your business and keep it going for the long run. Technology can't do it for you.

As a self-employed business owner, you have to have a passion—and I don't just mean a passion for the work you do, whether it's designing websites, photographing weddings and babies, caring for pets, creating glass art, etc. You also need to have a passion for *business itself.* You need to have a passion for *being an entrepreneur*, and for doing the things that will keep your business going.

I paraphrase Woody Allen in this book: "Eighty-two percent of success is showing up." Whether you choose to run your self-employed business from a home office or a downtown skyscraper, you must be willing to "show up" for work *every single day!* This means not only creating new products to sell, or getting work done for your clients. It also means calling or emailing new prospects, writing an eNewsletter to keep in touch with old clients, planning your next marketing campaign, or doing whatever you need to do to succeed and keep your business going.

Technology can help you automate many of these tasks, but it can't provide you with the passion to get things done. If you don't have a passion for entrepreneurship, it will be very hard for you to create a successful business.

It's also important to remember there's a flip-side of technology that's bad for business. Along with all the innovations we've had in the past decade, technology has also created more distractions. Ten years ago, you could spend hours surfing the Internet, or posting on online message boards, or be distracted by checking your email every five minutes. These days, there's Facebook, YouTube, Instagram, Snapchat, online games, texting, tweeting, etc.

To be a successful business owner, you have to be able to *focus your attention* on your business. You have to prioritize and organize, to get your work done in a timely manner, and to get the most important work done first. If you let all the daily distractions take you away from what you *should* be doing, your business will never be as successful as it should be. This was important ten years ago, and due to the increase in distractions, it's even more important today.

There's one more thing that hasn't changed in ten years. As a small-business owner, you need to be able to sell—sell your products, sell your services, or sell yourself as a skilled consultant or just a trustworthy business person. Maybe you hate selling. But if you don't do it, your business will be in jeopardy, and your chances of success will be minimal.

Technology can *help* you to sell, but it can't do the selling *for* you. For example, you can post articles on your blog to establish yourself as an expert in a certain industry (business consulting, application design, etc.), and to drive content to your website. But you still need to *write* those articles yourself and do the work of posting them on your blog. There is advice on how to become an effective salesperson later in the book.

People buy from people, and they buy more often from people they trust. It's up to you to reach out to your clients and customers and establish that trust. It's not about you. It's about your customers and how you can serve their needs.

Can you do it? Can you become an entrepreneur and build a successful business? That's up to you. Remember, the subtitle of this book is, *Is Self-Employment for You?* Only you can answer that question. This book is designed to *help* you find the answer to that question.

If you decide to go into business after reading this book, that's great! Terrific! Outstanding! I wish you success! But if you decide *not* to go into business after reading this book, that's fine too. There's nothing wrong with continuing to work your 9-to-5 job. But the fact that you've bought this book means you're at least *thinking* about starting your own business, and wondering, "Is self-employment the right choice for you?"

So let's get started on answering that question.

Preflight Checklist

THE 10 STEPS TO THINK LIKE AN ENTREPRENEUR

Step #1: What kind of entrepreneur are you?

If you're thinking about transitioning into self-employment, the first question you should ask yourself is "What kind of entrepreneur should I be?"

You will be in a stronger position to succeed if you first commit to *being an entrepreneur*. That is, you must commit yourself to the *business of entrepreneurship*. The kind of business you pick is secondary to wanting to live the lifestyle of an entrepreneur.

From what I've observed, the decision-making process for the most successful entrepreneurs goes something like this:

❏ After working for others many years, entrepreneurs can't view themselves doing their current jobs for the rest of their lives. Self-employment becomes the only option. They want control over their destinies. The thought of independence and what that will bring becomes their passion.

❑ Once they make the decision to start their own businesses, real entrepreneurs don't look back. They methodically go about looking for businesses that will help them to succeed over the long run. They are not looking for the next get-rich-quick opportunity. They approach the process of selecting a business in a very pragmatic way.

❑ For several years, I hosted "Small Business Innovators," a local radio show in Seattle, where I interviewed hundreds of successful entrepreneurs about their business strategies. One thing all my interviewees have in common is that they *think* like entrepreneurs. Their eyes and ears are always open to new opportunities.

Step #2: What's your niche?

The key to developing a successful small business is to find a niche. You want to solve a problem for your customers that no one else is solving—or solve it in such a way that it makes it more convenient or a better value for them to come to you, rather than one of your competitors. You want to make your business all about *your customers* and *their needs*, not about you.

A few years ago, I had a call on my radio show from a man in Santa Ana, CA who said he wanted to open a t-shirt shop in nearby Venice Beach, CA. He had particular passages and quotes that he wanted to display on the t-shirts. This was his passion.

I've been to Venice Beach many times. In my opinion, the last thing the town needs is another t-shirt shop. On the Venice Beach waterfront, t-shirts typically sell two-for-$5. I told my caller, if he chose this path, he'd have an abundance of competition and it would be a tough business to build.

I asked him what he was currently doing for a living. He said he drove for UPS, and during our conversation, he revealed that he knew every retail store, office complex, street, and back alley in the greater Santa Ana area.

I suggested that his geographical knowledge could be very profitable to him, since Santa Ana is home to many retirees, thanks to its warm climate. He might invest in a used para-transit bus and start up a "Concierge Service" to transport retirees throughout the Santa Ana area. His target audience could be the "sandwich generation"—adults in their fifties and sixties who have both children and elderly parents in their care. Many of these people work full-time and can't always spare the time to transport their older parents to places they need to go. Wouldn't it be great if there was a local shuttle that could take their parents to doctor's appointments, the shopping mall, card games, the movies, etc.?

I don't know if my caller ever pursued this concept. There may have been restrictions to starting this type of shuttle service. And who knows! Another entrepreneur may have already cornered the "transportation service for retirees" market in Santa Ana. But the point is, that's the way real entrepreneurs think. Instead of trying to start a dime-a-dozen business, they look to see where there is a niche they can fill, a problem they can solve, and build a business concept based on that.

Step #3: Finding a niche within a niche

In developing their business, good entrepreneurs don't stop with just finding a niche. They look for a niche within a niche (or a "2X niche") or even a niche within a niche within a niche (or a "3X niche," if you will). Finding a 2X niche or a 3X niche allows you to target more specific customers and helps you to set your business apart from competitors in your industry.

For example, a graphic design business is a niche. If you want to provide graphic design services to local non-profits, that's a niche within a niche. If you want to provide graphic design services to local *arts-based* non-profits (e.g., art museums, community arts forums, youth symphonies), medical nonprofits (e.g., blood banks, cancer research centers), or nonprofits that provide services to the elderly (e.g., "Meals On Wheels"), those are 3X niches.

~

Try to develop several types of niches to set your business apart from your competitors.

~

Sometimes you have to "dig deep" to find a 3X niche that will give you a profitable target market. For example, say you are a building contractor who specializes in upgrading commercial buildings to make them compliant with the Americans with Disabilities Act. In other words, you and your workers typically add access ramps, chair lifts, and other features to the exteriors and interiors of office buildings to make them wheelchair accessible. (This is your 2X niche.)

One day, you read an article in *Modern Maturity*, the magazine of the AARP (American Association of Retired Persons), which states that many older adults (i.e., ages 75 and older) want to stay in their homes as long as possible before moving to a retirement community. This is called "aging in place." You realize your contracting firm could provide home remodeling services to this target audience. You can make homes wheelchair accessible by widening doorways and retrofitting bathrooms, and there are so many things you can do with lighting, carpets, ramps, countertops, chairs, etc., to help older adults stay in their homes longer. Congratulations!

You've found your 3X niche!

Real entrepreneurs often develop a 2X niche or a 3X niche based on something that happened to them personally. I once interviewed a woman who had built a business around helping adult children find resources and housing alternatives for their aging parents. She had discovered this business concept through her experiences with her own elderly mother.

When her mother was becoming frail and forgetful, this entrepreneur had many questions about how to provide the best care for her: Would her mother be eligible for Medicare? Would Medicare cover the cost of nursing homes for individuals with dementia? What is Medicaid, and would her mother be eligible for it? How would you go about selecting a long-term care facility? Would she need an attorney to handle her mother's legal or financial affairs? What's the difference between "power of attorney" and "durable power of attorney?" Did her mother even need a nursing home, or would an adult family home or retirement center be more suitable?

My interviewee had looked around for an advisor who could help her to navigate the questions and problems that a primary caregiver must face when caring for an aging adult. But she discovered there were no such advisors. She was basically on her own.

Then she started thinking like an entrepreneur. She said to herself, "I couldn't be the only person trying to navigate through these difficult choices." She started a business that linked adult children to resources for aging parents. Now, she counsels adult children on how to navigate the process of selecting a nursing home or adult family home for their aging parents. She assists people in submitting state and federal government paperwork and connects them with lawyers who specialize in living wills and powers of attorney. She is a prime example of an individual who found a niche and began solving problems for her clients.

Step #4: The free agency perspective

As a self-employed business owner, I operate under what I call the free agency perspective. Being a free agent basically means you are in business for yourself, even if you happen to work for other people. It means you're always trying to do your best possible work on your current project and looking for your next project as well. You're in the service of many, but your devotion is to yourself and your family.

By the power invested in me, I hereby declare you a "free-agent." You are now: *Your Name, Inc.* So grab a piece of paper and your full name followed by "Inc." Keep it in close proximately, so you can constantly remind yourself and refer back to this piece of paper frequently.

"Free agency" is not just another catch phrase to describe the entrepreneurial spirit. The self-employed free agent is the "Undercover Agent" of the business world, working for several clients at once, instead of one single employer. These clients can include everyone from individual customers to small and medium-sized businesses.

Self-employed free agents have the freedom to conduct their business anytime, anywhere, often beneath the clumsy and predictable radar of Big Business. They aren't hampered by the outdated business models, lack of effective communication, and slow decision-making processes that often plague large companies.

In fact, the corporate disadvantages that slow the progress of Big Business often work to the advantage of self-employed free agents. Many large companies will pay self-employed free agents to perform specialized tasks that they themselves can't handle. Self-employed free agents are comfortable in the age of rapid information exchange and can conduct business with a speed and efficiency that large companies can't achieve.

The self-employed free agent often works with other free agents. My own company has no employees, but at any given time, I employ up to seventeen part-time people of various wide-ranging skills to handle the needs of my clients. I refer to these people as "free agents," never as "contractors" or "consultants."

Competition among self-employed free agents is varied and stimulating. It fosters a creative process and fair market trade that recalls a more meaningful time, when one person's ideas often became a reality. This is no dream or wishful thinking; it's a practical and very real way to do business. My free agency perspective has helped me to sustain a successful, independent business for over twenty-five years.

Step #5: The "Sharing Economy"

Since I first wrote *Is Self-Employment for You?* back in 2003, the free agency perspective has moved into new industries, such as transportation and hospitality. Free agents are now finding work or earning money by providing services that they couldn't or normally *wouldn't* have provided before the Internet age created these "alternative" types of businesses. Much of this is due to the "sharing economy."

In the "sharing economy," free agent owners of vehicles, rooms for rent, etc., use online resources to "share" their goods and services with potential customers. (Some economists argue that it should really be called the "access economy," since customers aren't actually "sharing" these resources, but paying to access them.) The companies that operate in the "sharing economy" are often called peer-to-peer businesses, since they use Web platforms and mobile apps to connect service providers with customers. Some examples are:

Uber—Uber provides transportation services, connecting drivers with people seeking rides in cities throughout the world. Customers use the Uber mobile app or website to request and schedule trips and to pay for trips using credit or debit card. Uber hires free agent drivers as independent contractors, and the drivers use their own vehicles to transport customers. The company has several classifications of cars and drivers, including UberX (everyday cars, driven by everyday drivers), UberBlack (town cars, such as Cadillacs), UberSUV, and UberTaxi (which features actual taxis). Founded less than a decade ago, Uber has become an unparalleled and unexpected success. The company is now valued at $50 billion, and provides services to fifty-eight countries and over 300 cities worldwide. (Some business writers even refer to the "sharing economy" as the "Uber economy," in the same way that people refer to Google when they talk about search engines, i.e., "I'll Google it.") Uber's success has spawned other transportation services where free agents provide the vehicles and do the driving, including Lyft, SideCar, and BlaBlaCar (the last being a long-distance, city-to-city ridesharing service, instead of an inter-city service). These transportation companies are now carrying more people than any cab company or limousine service, and yet they don't own or lease a single vehicle.

Getaround and RelayRides—These two services might be called "Airbnb for car rentals." (See below.) Using mobile and Web apps, customers can rent cars from free agent vehicle owners, and use them during the times when the owners are not using them (e.g., when the owners themselves are out of town).

Airbnb—A Web-based business that connects travelers with free agents offering short-term rentals in their homes, apartments, summer homes, or condos. The travelers book their rentals through Airbnb's website and can save money over a more expensive hotel or motel. Other vacation rental sites use the Airbnb model, such as VRBO (Vacation Rental By Owner), HomeAway, FlipKey, and Roomarama. (NOTE: VRBO is owned by HomeAway, which in turn is now owned by Expedia.)

Taskrabbit and Zaarly—These two businesses each offer a peer-to-peer marketplace to allow free agents to provide "odd job" services to others. Using mobile apps, customers can find free agents to help them with anything from stacking store shelves to home repair to computer repair to baking a pie.

DogVacay—Using this service, dog owners can leave their dogs at the home of a caretaker when they go on vacation. It's cheaper than a kennel, and may provide the dog with a more comfortable "vacation spot."

~ ~ ~

If you can use the "sharing economy" to help grow your business, more power to you. Just be aware that you need to handle "sharing economy" jobs with the same devotion and quality of service that you would give to any normal job of the same type. If you're an Uber driver, you have the flexibility to pick your own hours. But you still need to show up at the appointed time to pick up your customer and treat the customer with courtesy and respect.

If you're using Airbnb to rent out a second condo that you own to vacation renters, you need to make sure the condo has the amenities (i.e., towels, soap, shampoo, a coffee maker, Wi-Fi, cable TV) that your customers might expect to find at a regular hotel or motel. Also, you should make sure the condo is thoroughly cleaned (carpets vacuumed, bathrooms and kitchens scrubbed, bed sheets washed, etc.) after each guest departs, so it will be fresh and clean for the next guest who uses it. In short, run it as close to a Four Seasons Hotel experience as possible.

"Sharing economy" sites usually have rating systems where both the customer and the service provider receive star ratings. For example, Uber has a five-star rating system by which customers rate the services provided by their drivers. If a driver gets a rating lower than four stars from his or her customers, that driver can be expelled from Uber's systems, and Uber refuses to work with that individual anymore. However, the same applies (in theory, at least) to the Uber customer. If the customer exhibits bad behavior during the ride, the Uber driver can give him or her a low rating on the website. Uber can then refuse to provide rides for that individual.

On Airbnb's website, vacation renters can post reviews of the places they've stayed and of the hospitality services their hosts provided. This means, if you use Airbnb to offer your condo for short-term rental to vacationers, you need to consistently provide your guests with a clean and safe place to stay, and good service. If your previous guests post bad reviews of your condo or your services on Airbnb's website, other renters could pass you by in favor of rentals with better ratings.

Be aware that all is not rosy for workers in the "sharing economy." In particular, Uber has received a lot of bad press due to business practices against its drivers. For example, Uber has repeatedly slashed its fares to compete with other ridesharing and taxi services. Some Uber drivers are complaining that, with prices so low, it's become very hard for them to make a decent living wage. Since Uber drivers have to pay for their own gas, auto maintenance, and car insurance, some complain that they're actually *losing* money by working for Uber. Also, Uber discourages its passengers from tipping their drivers and claims on its mobile app that a "driver tip amount" is included in the regular fare. But Uber drivers in San Francisco have filed a lawsuit claiming that the company is pocketing this "tip amount" instead of paying it to drivers as they should.

(In the interest of full disclosure, I should confess that I do use Uber's services. However, I'm not sure I would ever want to do business with them, especially with their reputation for using bullying tactics against people who oppose them, e.g., investigating the private lives of journalists who criticize them. At the very least, I would recommend that if you do use Uber, you ignore their so-called "anti-tipping policy" and give your driver a good tip.)

Other "sharing economy" sites have received criticisms from free agents who use them to find work. For example, on Taskrabbit, workers must set an hourly rate for each type of job they're willing to do (e.g., household repairs, cleaning, gardening). As you might imagine, those who offer lower rates usually get more jobs. If you use Taskrabbit, you may end up getting $30/hour to do a job for which you would normally charge $50/hour. Also, while sites like Taskrabbit give you the flexibility to set your own schedule, the time you spend in doing a lower-paying Taskrabbit job may prevent you from taking on higher-paying work elsewhere.

Free agents have also reported problems with the worker ratings systems of peer-to-peer businesses. Workers on Taskrabbit have reported being penalized by Taskrabbit's metrics system for turning down jobs, even if they were unqualified to do the job. Uber drivers report that if their 5-star rating is suddenly lowered to 4.7 or 4.4, thanks to a single bad review from an irate passenger, Uber will suspend the driver's account. Meanwhile, passengers with 1.0 ratings are still receiving Uber service.

At this time, the parameters of the "sharing economy" are still being defined. Many peer-to-peer businesses are still working out the ways they work with free agents. My advice to you is to tread cautiously in dealing with these companies. They may be a source of quick and steady jobs for your business. But with the low prices they offer to their customers, you may end up working for lower pay, or worse, actually losing money by working for them. Don't let peer-to-peer businesses be your only source of income and, after you've worked a few jobs for Uber, Taskrabbit, or similar companies, examine what you've earned and what you've learned and make a decision if it's worth it for you to keep working with them.

Step #6: Corporate employment

The best thing about the free agency perspective is you don't have to be self-employed to adopt it. You can think of yourself a "free agent" even if you work for a mega-conglomerate, a corporation, a small business, in government service, or are unemployed. In fact, even if you ultimately decide not to start your own business and to stick with a full-time job, it's still a good idea to adopt the free-agent mentality.

It used to be that people would work for one company all their lives. They would be hired by that company just out of high school or college and work there until they retired. But job security is like the typewriter. It is a relic of the past.

Companies regularly lay off employees and eliminate jobs to cut costs and keep their stockholders happy. It's probable that you will make five or six job or career changes during your lifetime. This may not be fair, but if you accept this as the way things are, it becomes easier to see yourself in the free-agent mentality.

Today, you might be lending your expertise to Acme, Inc. as a full-time employee, for which you receive compensation in the form of a regular salary. As long as this arrangement remains mutually beneficial, your relationship will continue. Always give your best effort to the projects you handle for your current employer. Remember, you will always be judged by the success or failure of your most recent work.

As you work on each job or project, always be on the lookout for your "next gig." If you find a new project within your company, take it. If you look ahead and don't see a new project developing with that company, or if you see hard times and possible layoffs on the horizon, it might be a good idea to start looking around at new companies with new projects that might need your talents more.

~

**Even if you never start your own
business, adopting the free
agency perspective will give you
an advantage.**

~

As a free agent, you assume responsibility for your own success and wellbeing. If you accept that nothing is permanent in today's job market, it becomes easier to anticipate and prepare for the transition points in your career. You will no longer see your long-term success as being dependent on your current employer. Instead, you will see yourself as the ultimate master of your own destiny.

Step #7: Innovator vs Follower

When it comes to starting your own business, there are two kinds of entrepreneurs: The Innovator and the Follower. The Innovator is one who tries to sell a new concept, invention, or a new way of doing business. Bill Gates is an example of an Innovator. Forty years ago, almost no one had a computer, much less computer software, at home or in the office. Bill Gates and his contemporaries invented software that could be used by everyday people who had no training at all in computer programming. Another innovator of our time is Jeff

Bezos. Twenty years ago, the Internet was just starting to come into widespread use and was then used mostly for email and business transactions. With Amazon.com, Jeff Bezos introduced a new concept—that a product (in this case, books) could be sold to everyday consumers over the Internet.

Now he is exploring how to use drones for delivering packages.

A Follower is an entrepreneur who follows a tried-and-true, tested product or service, like an accounting firm, home-cleaning business, landscaping, or a plumbing enterprise. The foundation for this type of business has already been established, and the entrepreneur's major goal is to find his or her own niche. These types of businesses may not be sexy, but they typically succeed more often than the businesses started by Innovators. The Follower doesn't have to work as hard to establish the need for his or her product or service. The potential client or customer already knows the benefits of hiring a home cleaning or landscaping service or calling in a plumber to fix the sink.

Whether you're an Innovator or a Follower, but especially if you're an Innovator, the self-employed business mindset is a necessity. An Innovator faces the daunting task of trying to convince customers that they need this new product or service, even though they've never tried it before. It takes time to convince people to try something new and establish it in their minds so they keep coming back to it. During this time, you've got to keep yourself in business, which means using your time well and handling your finances responsibly as you seek out new clients, test and improve your product or service, and develop your customer base.

If you're a Follower, you don't face the struggle of introducing something new to your potential clients, but you still have the task of convincing them they should do business with you. Even if they've used your type of product or service before, they are more likely to do business with a well-established company than with a free agent who is just starting out. It may take you a while to locate the clients in your area who need your exact product or service. Or you may find you have to make adjustments to your business, because the demand for your product or service is not as strong as you thought it would be.

Step #8: Dull is good

If you've ever watched any movies or TV shows about the high-tech world—*The Social Network*, for example, or the HBO series, *Silicon Valley* or the AMC series *Halt and Catch Fire*—you might get the impression that starting a small business is a high-pressure affair. These "tech movies" and "tech shows" usually focus on a collection of nerds and corporate cast-offs at a start-up company who are trying to be the first ones out with some high-tech innovation, or Internet phenomenon, or computer game. Usually, these tech guys are trying to reach the "Promise Land" of fame and fortune. They are looking to score million-dollar deals from venture capitalists, and in the course of a single episode, they may win and/or lose funding from some "angel investors." Or maybe they come up with an idea for an impressive new high-tech program right before a big "Tech World" trade show, and the nerds have to spend forty-eight straight hours writing computer code to get the program ready in time for the show.

At any rate, these "tech shows" give you the idea that all startup businesses are high-risk ventures, and that you must be a super-innovative genius and live a stressful, anxiety-driven lifestyle in order to succeed. Well, that may be how things are in the fast-paced high-tech world of Silicon Valley (and it certainly makes for good drama on television). But for the vast majority of small business start-ups, this is not the case.

~

Over 80% of businesses that succeed would be defined by the media as dull.

~

You don't read about them or see them on TV, but you pass by them every day in your car. They have had an "Open For Business" sign literally or figuratively posted outside for decades. Gordon Gekko in *Wall Street* said: "Greed, for lack of a better word, is good."[1] In self-employment: "Dull is good."

Which isn't to say that you necessarily have to start a business where you do something dull, or spend your days doing boring work. It simply means your business idea doesn't have to be innovative. You can start a business as a marketing or PR consultant, caterer, home care provider, private tutor, window washer, dog walker, etc., if any of these interest you.

And while you do have to work hard to make your business a success, you don't have to live a high-stress lifestyle. When you're just starting out, you may have to put in a good deal of extra work (i.e., working weekends, staying an extra two hours at the end of the day to get things done). But if you are organized and dedicated to your business, it doesn't have to be a constant high-stress job. Over time, your business will get easier. When it becomes more routine, it will usually become more successful. It's better to spend several years developing an "ordinary" but sustainable business that will hopefully be successful for the next decade or two than to "kill yourself" in a high-stress job trying to invent a new innovation that will enable you to score a million-dollar deal.

---

[1] *Wall Street*, dir. Oliver Stone, perf. Michael Douglas, Charlie Sheen, Daryl Hannah, Martin Sheen, and Hal Holbrook (United States: Twentieth Century Fox Film Corporation, 1987), DVD.

Step #9: Quick buck? Go to Vegas.

In a world where a traditional career path no longer exists, where it has become normal for people to make five or six career changes in one lifetime, starting your own business may be the best way to achieve security for yourself and your family. But be aware, it will take time! You can't expect to establish security as a self-employed business owner overnight.

~

Starting a successful business is not about making a quick buck.

~

Actually, the quest to make fast money is contrary to starting a long-term, successful business. It goes against building relationships with your clients and competitors and tinkering with your concept over time. The more money you risk trying to get rich quick, the more money you can lose.

Yesterday, I heard a radio commercial from an "instant wealth guru" who was selling a book and CD on how to get rich in the real estate market. He claimed there was absolutely no risk involved and promised you would be wealthy within one year if you used his magical moneymaking formula. The word "R-I-C-H" was even part of the phone number you needed to call to purchase his training course. Whether it's real estate, a can't-miss direct marketing scheme, or a video that will make you an overnight positive thinker, we are deluged with infomercials, books, and CDs telling us how we can reverse our misfortunes instantly. I strongly urge you to resist these get-rich temptations. The only people who get rich selling videos and books with this "quick-wealth" approach are the people hawking the schemes.

As a self-employed business owner, your mindset should be geared toward establishing a long-term business that will provide security for you and your family in good times and bad. It may take several years (e.g., three to five), depending on your product or service, to build your business and make it profitable. But once you've established that business, it may be profitable enough to provide you with better financial security than any job you've had before. If instant money is your goal, your odds are better in Las Vegas.

Step #10: The dot-com crash

When I first wrote *Is Self-Employment for You?* back in 2003, America was just coming out of a recession, which had been our "hangover" from the economic boom of the 1990s. A few elements had caused the 2000–2001 recession, but one of the major factors was the "dot-com crash." In the first two years of the 21st century, a number of dot-com start-ups that had prospered in the '90s suddenly went bust and faded into Internet history.

It's been over a decade since the "dot-com crash." You might think I'd be "digging up old fossils" from the early days of the Internet to talk about it now. But the fact is, the failure of the dot-coms taught many business people, including me, some valuable lessons. And those lessons are still relevant for business owners and entrepreneurs today.

In the mid-1990s, the Internet was seen as "the next big thing," a better and faster way to do business, trade goods and services, and move information. As Internet access became available to almost everyone, "dot-com start-ups" became one of the most popular entrepreneurial businesses. It began with Jeff Bezos who started Amazon.com as an online bookseller in his backyard garage. From then on, if something could be sold, traded, or transacted over the Internet, an entrepreneur would find a way to do it.

As long as the economy was good, investors and venture capitalists were more than willing to pour billions of dollars into dot-coms, hoping to cash in on the so-called "New Economy." But when the national economy started to cool down, many investors stopped putting their money into dot-coms that were spending millions of dollars a day and still not turning a profit. By the time many businesses realized they were on the wrong course, the debt was too high and the only alternative was to close the doors. When the "dot-com bubble" burst, investors lost billions of dollars, and many of the dot-coms became jokingly (and sadly) referred to as "dot-gones."

Even if you don't plan to start an Internet-based business, you can still learn a lot about what *not* to do as a self-employed business owner by studying the mistakes of the dot-com era. If the burst of the dot-com bubble teaches us anything, it's that even "New Economy" businesses must still obey "Old Economy" rules.

Again, Rule #1 is "A business must eventually take in more money than it spends." When all is said and done, the Internet is nothing more than an extremely useful communications tool. An Internet-based business must *still* offer a tangible product or service and must still make an actual profit if the business is to survive.

What are some of the reasons the dot-coms failed? Let me count the ways:

❑ They used other people's money (that is, money given to them by investors) and lots of it. When you use other people's money to build your business, it becomes frighteningly easy to spend. You develop bad habits, such as not accounting for each dollar. Also, when someone else is financing you, you don't have that sense of urgency to make your business successful and profitable as soon as possible. That's what I mean when I say there is such a thing as having too much money when you start your business.

❑ The idea behind many dot-coms was to build businesses based on the novelty of Internet technology, not on the product or service being offered. Many dot-com entrepreneurs were not interested in offering a quality product or service, but in how they could leverage that product or service into quick money or an IPO.

❑ Many dot-coms tried to "conquer the world" with their products or services before they really understood it or before they had fully tested their concepts. They spent millions of advertising dollars trying to capture "market share"—that is, trying to outdo their competitors to be the top search engine, or ISP, or online toy seller on the Internet, when they hadn't yet perfected their concepts or their services or figured out how to turn them into profitable enterprises.

❑ In many cases, dot-coms invested money in unnecessary expenditures, such as high salaries, lavish office furniture, and elaborate corporate events.

❑ Many dot-com CEOs were overnight wonder kids in their 20s who lacked the *perspective* and *experience* it takes to start a successful business. A few more people with gray hairs around the water cooler would have helped enormously.

~ ~ ~

Now I have a confession to make. I wasn't immune to the "gold rush mentality" of the dot-com era. In the late 1990s, I had more "disposable" income than at any other time in my life. I invested some of my money in dot-coms, but my investments were very limited because I was always skeptical about the long-term success of many of these ventures. When these dot-coms later went out of business, I lost *some* money, but not much.

The first time I heard the term "Burn Rate" was at a stockholder's meeting in the year 2000, from the CEO of an Internet start-up I had invested in. I asked a fellow investor what the term meant. He said it was "the money that feeds the monthly cash flow to the negative, but which the company needs in order to brand its product in the marketplace, with the goal of bringing in new investors."

In other words, the company was furiously spending more money than it was making in an effort to attract investors with more money to spend. By bringing in new investors as quickly as possible, the company hoped to offset its massive business costs until it could establish itself enough to turn a profit. In doing this, the company had created a *corporate culture of losing money.*

Unfortunately, this company's investors, myself included, soon grew very tired of hearing about the "Burn Rate." In essence, the company was asking us to believe the concept "We're not losing money! We're just spending more than we earn as we move towards making a profit." (This is like an airline pilot telling the passengers, "Don't worry, folks! The plane is not crashing! It's just that the rate of descent is faster than we'd like!") As investors like myself stopped believing in the "Burn Rate" mentality, they stopped investing, and the company went out of business.

In their early days, Google and Facebook received a good deal of funding from venture capitalists despite being available as free services to all Internet users and having no real products to sell. Over time, both sites have worked out a way to produce income, largely through advertising. Google offers Search Engine Marketing (or SEM) through its AdWords program with which advertisers pay to have their "click ads" appear at the top of search engine results. Facebook offers social media advertising with which targeted "click ads" appear on the Facebook pages of people who may have an interest in some product or service (e.g., those who list their personal status as "engaged to be married" on their Facebook profiles may receive ads from local wedding photographers, dress designers, or caterers).

Advertisers flock to Google and Facebook now, because they know these are the two most-used sites on the Internet, so it's very likely their ads will be seen by people in their intended target audiences. But these sites are the *exceptions* to the rule. Other dot-coms that have no products to sell, or that offer their services for free, have had a harder time making money solely through advertising, because they don't receive as many "hits" per day as Google and Facebook and therefore are not as popular with advertisers. (At this writing, Twitter is still refining its business model by offering "Promoted Tweets" as a form of advertising to generate revenue.)

The point is, despite their overwhelming popularity in the (relatively) new world of the Internet, Google and Facebook still had to find a way to continue to exist according to "Old Economy" rules. Google has managed to provide tangible results for its investors, and at some point, Facebook is going to do the same. If you plan to start an online business, you need to consider very carefully what your business model will be and how your business will turn a profit. Don't expect the "wonder of the Internet" to carry you forever.

Preflight Checklist

THE 8 MYTHS OF
SELF-EMPLOYMENT

Myth #1: Entrepreneurs are huge risk-takers

Before we get into the ins and outs of self-employment, I want to take some time to dispel some of the more common myths about entrepreneurship. It's my opinion that these myths often act as an obstacle to would-be entrepreneurs, preventing them from starting their own businesses, or in some cases, from building successful, sustainable businesses.

The first myth, as stated above, is that entrepreneurs are huge risk takers. I've found that this is simply not true. The vast majority of successful entrepreneurs are risk-adverse. They are cautious, thoughtful, decisive, organized, focused, and pragmatic. They also possess the most important trait of all: good judgment. They dream, but they are not dreamers.

Our media culture glorifies the small business owners who took big risks and "made it big"—which isn't surprising, because it makes a great story. How many times have you read the story about someone who came up with an innovative invention or business idea, started his or her business on a credit card, and has now become a "master of the business world?" (Don't be seduced by this approach. Financing your business on a credit card is not just risky—it's reckless!)

The media never does interviews with the "typical small business owner." They never do a story about, say, someone who started his own house cleaning service, or dog walking service, or catering business, because these ideas don't have the same "sparkle of success and innovation" that you get from, say, selling hydroelectric cars or inventing a new online retail business. But many small business owners who have these types of businesses—marketing consultants, graphic and Web designers, family portrait photographers, wedding and party planners, interior decorators, private tutors, life coaches, child care or senior care providers, etc.—are running very profitable businesses. They are the ones who seem to be gone a lot. That's because the business owner and family are off visiting their European villa.

~

True entrepreneurs believe that the *real* risk in life is working for someone else.

~

You can be laid off or fired at any moment. If you can hit that glorious point when your business is steady and profitable, you have reached the "Promised Land." You aren't in a hurry to make big money in a short time frame either. You realize that being an entrepreneur is a lifestyle that you will be comfortable in for a very long time.

Myth #2: Smalls businesses fail because they are undercapitalized

There's a common misperception that start-up businesses fail because they don't have enough money. In my experience, the opposite is true.

~

Many start-ups fail because they have *too much money!*

~

(Yes, you read that right.)

In the dawn of your business, all you have going for you are concepts. If you don't have a lot of money sitting around, you can't blow it. Your overall goal is to keep your business going until it becomes profitable. Start-ups with little money are more likely to spend it wisely and carefully. They keep careful track of their budgets and expenses, employ low-cost marketing campaigns, and try not to take on any unnecessary expenditures.

On the other hand, start-ups with a lot of money are less careful with it. If they get a generous infusion of cash from a rich uncle or angel investors, they may feel obliged to do more, be more, spend more, and grow faster. They try to maximize their business and make it as big as possible, when they should be keeping expenditures to an absolute minimum until the business is more established. Many well-funded start-ups are notorious for spending themselves into oblivion while trying to establish themselves as big players in the marketplace, when they're just not ready for prime time.

I've personally seen entrepreneurs fail in their ventures for having too much money. About the time I first started my business, a colleague of mine started her own public relations firm. She opened her doors with beautiful offices in a prime location and had a good-sized staff to help launch her firm. Her wealthy father was financing most of her start-up costs.

I'll admit I was a bit jealous of her. I'd started my own business in a one-person office located in a building owned by publishers that printed my newspaper. As long as I printed my newspaper at that location, I was provided free office space. The office was not very nice (actually it was a rat hole but again it was free). The arrangement lasted for about ten years. Can you imagine the overhead I saved over a ten-year span? More on this later. At the time, I'd have given anything to have the financial resources that my colleague had.

I fully expected her public relations firm to be successful. She was (and is) an extremely bright person, and was well connected in the community. Prior to starting my newspaper, I'd used her firm to do publicity for a volunteer project I was working on for a small organization.

But, once more, her problem turned out to be too much overhead. I don't know exactly what her monthly expenses were, but they had to be quite high. Office rent was at least $5,000–7,000 per month. Add another $50,000 per month for salaries, and you can see the trouble coming. If her minimum overhead was $60,000 per month, that comes to over $700,000 per year in the first year.

She had landed a major client for her firm and was counting on that client to launch her business out of the starting gate. But that client fell through. Not long after that, a recession set in and there weren't too many new clients around who were looking for public relations work. As you can probably guess, her business soon folded.

In the years since this happened, I've learned a lot about running a business. Looking back, I think I was lucky that I didn't start out with a ton of money to finance my entrepreneurship. If I'd had the same financial resources as my colleague, I probably would have done exactly what she did. I might have started my own small business with several employees, high-profile office space, and lots of expenses.

And I might very well have lost that same business later on, when those expenses started to get out of hand.

As it was, I started out with very little money and had to work very hard to keep my business going. In the long run, this turned out to be a blessing. I've known of numerous entrepreneurs whose lives were too easy and who therefore did not feel they had to work as hard in order to make their businesses succeed. In the end, this may have cost them their businesses.

Myth #3: The first thing you need is a business plan

About once a week, I hear or see a so-called "business guru" saying, *When you start a business, the first step is to write your business plan.* My first impression is, this guy has never run a business. A business plan is the *last* thing you need to do.

The first thing you need to do is to make sure that your business concept has a fighting chance. If you don't, there is not a business plan designed that will save you. If you are curious about what I am talking about, I urge you to skip ahead right now to what I consider to be the most important step of setting yourself up for success.

While I think it's important to have a business plan, I also believe that business gurus place too much importance on having one and sticking to it.

~

A business plan is just a giant wish list.

~

You are projecting how you *hope* things will perform. In the real world, you never know how well your business will actually function until you open up your doors for business, and start trying to bring in the customers.

This is not to say that business plans are useless. Writing a plan for your business can give you a sense of what you want to accomplish, and where you want your business to be in a year, or five years. But I strongly recommend that you don't become a slave to your business plan. Many times, when you're just starting out, business plans keep you from doing what you *should* be doing. I've talked with people who were thinking of starting their own businesses but who never got past the "business plan" stage.

I recently heard from a friend who lost his regular job: "I want to start my own private practice as an architect." I think my friend would have a very good chance of starting a successful business. He has plenty of experience and also has many of the emotional and personality traits necessary for a self-employed business owner. But my friend is such a slave to continuous planning that he absolutely *refuses* to start his practice without first mapping out a long-term business strategy for himself. And yet, he never seems to be able to sit down and write out a business plan. He is avoiding what he feels is a crucial step to starting his own business.

My advice would be, "The hell with the business plan! You need clients for your architecture practice! Get on the phone and start making it happen!" But I'm betting my friend will not start his own business at this time, even though he's in a perfect position to do so. He will go out and find a new permanent position that he hopes will be more secure than his last job.

The mindset of the self-employed business owner requires *flexibility*, and a willingness to change tactics when things don't go your way. Business plans have a tendency to become outdated very quickly. The most important thing is to find a business that is functional.

For example, after six months in business, you may discover that you should be looking for a different kind of clientele, or that your marketing plan is flawed and needs to be reworked. It's better to change your goals and adjust your strategies than to stubbornly stick to a business plan that isn't working for you. If I've learned anything as a self-employed business owner, it's that there's no one "right way" to start a successful business.

Myth #4: "The customer is always right"

You've often heard the expression, "The customer is always right." This sounds like a noble goal, but for the self-employed, it's simply not true.

The maxim of "The customer is always right" was created primarily for the restaurant and retail industries—and it's in these industries that this maxim works best. The motto expresses the idea that customer service is top priority and that customers *must* be satisfied. So if a restaurant customer doesn't like his meal, the waiter should allow him to select a new entrée. If a customer buys a dress and then suddenly decides she doesn't like the color, she must be allowed to return or exchange it. Even when the customer is wrong, he or she is "always right."

~

But for self-employed business owners, the concept of "the customer is always right" should be taken with a grain of salt.

~

Of course, you should always try to do the best job possible and satisfy your clients in every way. If a client has a reasonable complaint, you should address it immediately and make corrections to satisfy him or her. If the client wants something done a certain way (e.g., "We *must* include this concept in our marketing campaign"), you must be flexible and creative enough to accommodate the individual. Always make sure you give the client your best possible product or service.

But the fact is, the customer is *not* always right. I estimate that about 80 percent of the people I encounter in business are a pleasure to work with, 10 percent are indifferent, and the other 10 percent are "high maintenance" clients. It's this last 10 percent that you need to be aware of.

High-maintenance clients are the customers/clients who *think* they are always right and are never satisfied with your product or service. They don't trust you to do the job they hired you for, because they think *they* can do it better. They insist on doing things "their way," even when you can suggest a more effective way to get something done. And they question the cost and necessity of everything you do for them.

Your best strategy is to simply avoid working with such clients. Trust me, you will save yourself plenty of mental and financial frustration if you choose not to work with high-maintenance business people. It may be hard to turn these clients down when you're just starting out and need the business. Sometimes, it seems as if you must take on the "devil's client" to get the money you need for next month's rent.

One of my major reasons for owning my own business is

freedom of association. I want the freedom to choose which clients I'll work with, and which clients I will turn down. I must say, however, it's a pleasure to work with the 80 percent of people who are *not* "high-maintenance." Most people *want* you to succeed and will help you to succeed if you're doing business with them. Seek those people out and avoid the rest as much as you can.

High maintenance customers/clients can suck the energy right of you and your business. Worse, they may not pay for your services and could cost you your business. That has happened to me twice.

Myth #5: Your competitors are your enemies

There's an age-old business attitude that says your competitors are not to be trusted. After all, they're in the same business as you, so why shouldn't they want to see you fail. They're out to steal your clients, steal your trade secrets, or otherwise damage your business, so you should avoid contact with them and watch them like a hawk.

In fact, just the opposite is true.

~

Competitors are your best friends!

~

They validate your business concept and keep you sharp and on top of your game. For example, if you were the only accountant in the world, potential customers would have a hard time understanding why they'd ever need your services. In all likelihood, they'd be happy doing their own accounting because there wouldn't be a precedent established to do it any other way.

If you're thinking of opening your own accounting firm, you'll have an easier time marketing your services, because all the other successful accounting firms have already laid a foundation for you to build on. This doesn't mean every potential client you approach will want to use *your* accounting service, but at least the average business owner understands the advantages of having an accountant. If you fail, don't blame your competitors.

When I first started my business, I thought my newspaper directed to older adults was an innovation. The older adult market had long been ignored in news publishing, and I thought I could change that. Of course, I didn't have to convince potential advertisers that *newspapers* would be a valid medium for reaching their markets. *The New York Times*, *The Wall Street Journal*, and millions of other newspapers that have been in circulation around the globe for centuries had already done that for me.

I did, however, have a problem communicating my vision for my *own* newspaper to potential advertisers. My core advertising targets included travel agencies, retirement centers, financial institutions, estate-planning attorneys, bookstores, health care facilities, and technology companies that catered to the older population. My publication was targeted to a very specific demographic that made up the clientele for these businesses. I thought there was no reason why they *shouldn't* want to advertise in my newspaper!

I've since learned that these businesses didn't trust my newspaper because it was so new. The concept of a newspaper published specifically for an older population had never been successfully tested before. Many of my advertising targets were unwilling to commit their marketing budgets to a brand new newspaper that was still building its audience.

"No, we'll just stick with the daily newspaper for now," they often told me. Advertisers were more willing to trust a newspaper like *The Seattle Times,* which has been in circulation for over 100 years and has a well-established readership. Another typical response was, "Older people are very set in their ways. They're not going to look around for a new newspaper to read."

To top it off, at the same time I began publishing my newspaper, two other publications aimed at older adults were starting up. One was based locally, one based out of state, but both were very similar to my operation. *With three newspapers going after the same local market and potential advertisers, I* thought, *there just isn't room in this town for all of us.*

I was almost ready to throw in the towel. But being a stubborn person, I kept pushing. Soon, I was selling enough ads to cover my own costs. The other publications targeting older adults were going after the same advertisers. They'd win a few and I'd win a few. I often looked at their ads and thought bitterly of all the advertisers I could have had in my paper if it weren't for them.

But over time, I slowly realized that my competitors were actually *validating* what I was trying to do. The presence of *three* newspapers for the older adult market started to convince the local business community that it was essential to have publications that catered to the needs of older adults.

I began looking at my competitors in a different way. I perused their publications for editorial ideas and possible advertisers. After reading one of my competitor's newspapers, I often said to myself, "I'd never have thought of going after *that* type of advertiser—but I will now!" I also realized that when all was said and done, I needed about thirty-five to forty ads in an average issue to make a pretty good living. Since there were *thousands* of potential advertisers in the area, the last thing I needed to worry about was my competitors stealing my business.

I soon became the cheering section for my competitors. I hoped their publications *would* succeed and their readers would respond well to their advertising. When I called on a potential client who'd had a good experience with a competitor's publication, my sales pitch became a lot easier.

My competitors and I each did little things to try to gain a competitive edge. In doing so, we all became stronger publications. I was the first to feature color photos in my newspaper. The other publications soon followed. One of my competitors had a strong local editorial content. I followed his example, adding the same type of content to my newspaper.

One of the publications died within a couple of years, because of high overhead. I knew they were selling about the same amount of advertising that I was, but I could also see that they were spending too much money on expensive office space and a large staff. They had an editor, photographer, sales manager, graphics artist, layout person, and a few more employees. I had a staff of one person: me! This was also an out-of-state publication, and I think this hurt them a bit, since they could only provide their readership with out-of-state perspectives on local events and concerns.

I wasn't sorry to see this publication go, because most of their advertisers did not have a good experience with them. The other competing publication was locally owned, and the publisher, like me, kept his overhead expenses low. But even though one of these publications ultimately failed, my competitors and I still established a precedent. Together, we proved there was a market for newspapers aimed at the older population. For the *niche market* publications that follow us, it will be much easier to prove to potential clients the value of advertising in such publications. They can point to our example and say, "Look! These fellows did it! So can we!"

Myth #6: If you have it in writing, it's guaranteed

I'm not suggesting here that you shouldn't draw up contracts or put agreements in writing. A contract or written agreement lays out the terms of your service to a customer. In most cases, the companies and clients you work with will be ethical and will have no problem honoring the terms of that contract, provided you do the same.

But be careful who you work for and work with.

~

If your client has a problem with ethics, a signed contract will not be enough to protect you from expensive litigation.

~

In the vast majority of instances, even if you win the case, you will end up not seeing one penny. And for a small business owner, a frivolous lawsuit from a bad client can be expensive or even fatal to your business. I speak from experience on this. Many years ago, I was contacted by a non-profit organization that wanted my help in developing radio commercials for a major ad campaign. When I spoke to the non-profit's director, he explained that he would be using other advertising mediums in addition to radio in this campaign. The non-profit director mentioned that he had recently appeared on a *The Oprah Winfrey Show* and that he would use Oprah's name and likeness in a billboard ad campaign ("As seen on *Oprah* …").

There was just one problem. The non-profit director mentioned that he hadn't actually contacted Oprah for permission to use her name and likeness on a billboard endorsing his organization. He really didn't think that was necessary. "As long as she doesn't object," he told me, "there's no problem."

That statement set off a warning bell in my mind. My gut instinct told me there was something wrong with the director's sense of business ethics. But instead of turning them down, I decided to take the non-profit on as a client. I worked with them and developed a successful radio ad campaign for the organization.

Then I sent the non-profit an invoice for the ad campaign. The non-profit director sent me a check for $50,000 but indicated that this money was intended for the *next* radio ad campaign I would develop for them. Except they hadn't yet paid me for their *first* radio ad campaign! I cashed the $50,000 check and used it to pay the radio stations that had run the commercials for the non-profit's first campaign.

The non-profit director was furious! He filed a lawsuit against me, claiming a breach of contract and misappropriation of funds. He later dropped the lawsuit (or at least he didn't pursue it). The last I heard, this director was being investigated for fraud and mismanagement of contributions to his organization. But it still cost me over $10,000 in legal fees, and a whole lot of aggravation, to defend myself against the lawsuit.

Since then, I've made it a point to always trust my gut instinct. It saves me a lot of trouble when it comes to avoiding bad clients and the possible legal problems I might have with them. If anything seems wrong about a potential client's morals, I'll walk away from the deal (or at least get the money up front). A signed contract is a good thing to have, but you shouldn't rely too much on it as a guarantee of your client's ethics.

Myth #7: Thinking positive is a key to success

There's a billion-dollar industry developed around the concept that thinking positively will change an outcome from bad to good or that if you always think positively good things will happen to you. I hate to sound like a "Debby Downer," but this is a ridiculous philosophy, especially if you're starting your own business.

There's nothing wrong with thinking positively, but sometimes it will help you more to think negative. The important thing is to be *realistic* about the problems you're facing and about how to handle them.

A friend once told me this story: "A man is out on the ocean in a sailboat, but his boat is not moving. Is he an optimist, a pessimist, or a realist? If he's an optimist, he says, 'Well, maybe the wind will pick up later today.' If he's a pessimist, he says, "Darn it, I'm going to be stuck out here all night, because there's no wind!" If he's a realist, he adjusts the sails."

You might have seen the movie *The Big Short* starring Brad Pitt, Christian Bale, Steve Carell, and others. It tells the true story of Michael Burry, Steve Eisman, Greg Lippmann, and other hedge fund managers who, in 2005, took a realistic look at the housing market and realized it was being driven by subprime mortgages, which were essentially bad loans.

These traders saw what no one else did—that these loans were a bad credit risk and would eventually fail. And so these traders began buying credit-default swaps on subprime mortgage bonds from the Big Banks (e.g., Lehman Bros., Goldman Sachs) that were selling the bad mortgages. Essentially, the hedge fund traders were buying insurance on mortgages that they knew were going to fail. The Big Banks were so caught up in the "easy money" they were making by selling these risky loans that they never realized the risk. They willingly sold credit-default swaps to the hedge fund traders, thinking these mortgages *did* start to fail. Beginning in 2007, the Big Banks were forced to pay insurance on the mortgages to the hedge fund traders, and the traders made a huge amount of money as the housing market collapsed.

Now, you may question the morals of traders who made millions by betting against the US economy, who saw an economic meltdown in the works and did nothing to prevent it. Had I been in their position, I would have shouted from the rooftops, "A financial disaster is coming! We need to take steps to stop this crisis before it happens!" Even if no one had listened to me, I could at least say I'd tried to warn them.

But the point is, these hedge fund traders did not succeed through positive thinking. They looked at the housing market and saw that it was based on smoke and mirrors. While everyone else was thinking positively and was sure that growth in the housing market would continue indefinitely, these traders were thinking *realistically*. They saw the debacle that was coming, and they took steps to ensure that when the housing bubble burst, they would not only survive but profit from it.

If you're a business owner, you should hope for the best but prepare for the worst. How can you prepare your business for a catastrophe similar to the 9/11 attacks? What can you do to prepare your business for the next recession or economic slowdown when it comes? (And it *will* come. The economy moves in cycles, alternately peaking and slowing every five to eight years or so.)

Of course, you shouldn't have a *negative attitude* as a business owner. When dealing with employees and customers, your persona should always be positive and optimistic. You must project confidence in what you're doing at all times.

But as a business owner, you must develop the ability to look at things *as they are*, not as you wish they were, and make decisions accordingly. You must continuously ask yourself, "What could go wrong?" and take steps to counter or prevent the negative outcomes. Thinking positive will not save your business from disaster. The smartest people in the room are always exploring the negatives or downsides of every decision they make.

Now for the biggest myth of all and is a logically sequenced after this myth about always thinking positive ... drum roll please ...

Myth #8: Follow your passion and the money will follow

Eighty percent of small businesses fail. One of the major reasons why the failure rate is so astonishingly high is that too many people buy into this long-held myth that *if you follow your passion, everything is going to work out okay.*

This idea is so prevalent that it seems to be included in *every* business success story you ever read or hear about. A few years ago, I saw an "entrepreneur mother" interviewed on a TV show talking about how she had built a home-based business into a very successful enterprise. She had been working as an attorney in a law firm in Portland, Oregon, and had taken six months off for maternity leave. As she was preparing her baby's room, she began looking around at various baby stores for wall stencils (animals, puffy clouds, birds, trees, etc.) that she could use to decorate the room. But the stencil packages she found were very overpriced. So she started her own mail order stencil company, offering low-priced stencils to expectant mothers.

At the end of the interview, the TV interviewer said, "So you followed your passion, and the money followed."

The entrepreneur looked a little startled and said, "Well, yes, if that's what you think I said."

The interviewer didn't get it. This "entrepreneur mother" didn't have a passion for creating stencils before she started her own business. What she did have was a passion for *being an entrepreneur.*

Stencil packages were just the opportunity she'd taken on. She found a niche based on her own personal experience and took the step of solving a problem for thousands of other parents (more on finding a niche later).

The problem with the statement "Follow your passion, and the money will follow" is that it promotes the *fantasy* of having your own small business, instead of the *reality*. It gives you the idea that if you start a business doing what you love to do, it will automatically be a success.

I don't mean to say you should start a business doing something that you hate to do. You should definitely do something that you enjoy. But never think that passion alone will be enough to sustain a business. The only thing that will keep you in business is *running your business AS a business,* not just as a hobby you enjoy.

I personally believe in the first part of the statement, but not the second part.

My own take on it is as follows:

~

"Follow your passion ... YES.
The money will follow ... MAYBE."

~

When I first started my business in 1988, I was not selling radio airtime for advertising, as I am now. I published a small-press newspaper aimed at the aging population. I had previously served as Executive Director of the Seattle chapter of the Alzheimer's Association and saw a need for this type of publication.

I'd been in the newspaper business for over six years and was still struggling. I gradually realized a *publication* was not the best venue for reaching my target audience. Many topics I was covering in my newspaper—travel, housing, financial planning, and hobbies such as golf—were not specific to the aging population. Potential advertisers would ask me why they shouldn't just advertise in the daily papers to reach the older adult population? The daily newspapers have travel, housing, financial planning, golf, and hobby sections as well and a much larger circulation. They had a good point and increasingly I had a hard time justifying my type of newspaper.

I approached a local radio station that catered to an older audience. The promos declared that it was the station for music from the '40s, '50s, and '60s. Tony Bennett, Frank Sinatra, Doris Day, and Elvis Presley, etc., were the headliners. If you've just turned forty, you probably have some nostalgia for music from the '90s. Same principal.

On weekends the station sold using a system called "block programming" with which radio time is sold for half-hour or one-hour periods, usually on Saturday and Sunday mornings. I purchased sixty minutes of airtime each week and produced and hosted my own show featuring the clients that were advertising in my newspaper. Now they were advertising over the broadcast waves.

I also learned a very important marketing lesson.

When I was publishing the newspaper, I had to create the content that I believed would be of value to older adults. There was a lot of guesswork involved. But with the radio format, the listeners would come to the station because of their love of the music. I didn't have to create the content. Frank Sinatra did that for me. (Thank you ol' Blue Eyes.) Also, the radio show was twice as profitable as the newspaper and took half the time.

We've all heard stories about the single mother on welfare who started a day-care-center and is now a multi-millionaire living on Park Avenue. It's the type of story that used to appear on *The Oprah Winfrey Show*. The *reason* this type of story is covered in the first place is because it *is* such an unusual and rare story.

The important thing to understand is: *Just because you are a great artist, it doesn't mean that you can run an art gallery. Just because your friends say you are a great cook, it doesn't mean that you can run a successful restaurant.*

Although you may be passionate about your business in the beginning, your passion will soon begin to wear thin when you deal with the realities of running a business. When I first started my weekly radio show, I really enjoyed the work. But after a while, it became like any other business. It's all about meeting deadlines and making sure your bank account is operating in the black.

I don't want to diminish your need or desire to do something that you enjoy. This can make the difference in being able to sustain a business for life. But again, *never confuse the dream with the reality.*

If, for example, your dream is to open an art gallery, the

reality will be choosing a good location, advertising, hosting promotional events to showcase new artists, making contacts within the local and national art communities, and showing up for work every day to earn enough to pay your rent and utilities. If your dream is to open an accounting or marketing service, the reality will be making cold calls every day to potential clients, advertising your services, attending local chamber of commerce meetings, paying your bills, and providing your clients with exceptional service that meets or exceeds their expectations.

These are the factors that will determine the success or failure of your business.

As for my radio show, it made money, certainly more than the newspaper but never as much as I would have liked. I decided to put the show on hiatus when a better opportunity came along. As part of my show, I had been buying radio airtime for my newspaper advertising clients. I received a call from the sales manager of a software company, asking me to purchase airtime for their own radio commercials. Soon, I was doing media buying for other companies who had not been connected with my newspaper or my radio show. Rather than running on one local station, I was now planning, creating, producing, and distributing radio commercials all over the United States and Canada. The prospects for professional and financial rewards were enormous. I was able to stay in radio, but in a much more successful venture than my newspaper or radio show had been. The money followed, but not in the way I'd expected.

Preflight Checklist

THE 5-MINUTE
SELF-EMPLOYMENT QUIZ

....

The 5-Minute Self-Employment Quiz is a questionnaire that will give you an idea of how good your chances are for successfully sustaining your small business.

Every one of its twenty questions has evolved from my personal experience as an entrepreneur and from interviewing hundreds of successful entrepreneurs for my book and on my radio shows.

The quiz takes about five minutes.

If you'd like, you can take it online on my website: www.selfemployquiz.com.

Instructions: Read the questions below and assign yourself a number between 1 and 10 in your answers. 1 is the lowest score and 10 is the highest. There should be few, if any, scores of 1 or 10 in your answers. Be completely honest and don't overthink your answers.

~ ~ ~

Question #1: Are you able to live without a steady paycheck?

Assign yourself a number between 1 ("I live paycheck to paycheck") and 10 ("A secure/steady paycheck is a myth"):

SCORE: 1—10 _____

Question #2: Do you or can you exercise good judgment?

Assign yourself a number between 1 ("I'm on my seventh marriage. Why is this relevant?") and 10 ("I have never made a mistake in my life"):

SCORE: 1—10 _____

Question #3: Are you flexible?

Assign yourself a number between 1 ("I cannot deviate from today's schedule") and 10 ("Let's solve this unforeseen problem—right now"):

SCORE: 1—10 _____

Question #4: Are you organized?

Assign yourself a number between 1 ("Where are my car keys?") and 10 ("My grocery list is organized by aisles"):

SCORE: 1—10 _____

Question #5: Are you decisive?

Assign yourself a number between 1 ("Not sure, maybe I am, let me think ... I don't know") and 10 ("Yes"):

SCORE: 1—10 _____

Question #6: Can you execute your projects?

Assign yourself a number between 1 ("My novel is only six years past due") and 10 ("Signed, sealed, and delivered"):

SCORE: 1—10 _____

Question #7: Can you sell yourself or product/service?

Assign yourself a number between 1 ("I hate selling and I just won't do it") and 10 ("I can sell ice cubes to Eskimos"):

SCORE: 1—10 _____

Question #8: Do you have ethics and integrity?

Assign yourself a number between 1 ("Who cares? Business is business") and 10 ("I will do what is right even if I lose money"):

SCORE: 1—10 _____

Question #9: Are you able to multitask?

Assign yourself number between 1 ("I am so confused. Too much coming at me") and 10 ("I am like a juggler at the circus"):

SCORE: 1—10 _____

Question #10: Are you competent with finances?

Assign yourself a number between 1 ("I don't know how I will pay my utility bill") and 10 ("On budget always"):

SCORE: 1—10 _____

Question #11: Can you handle adversity?

Assign yourself a number between 1 ("My day is ruined if I get a parking ticket") and 10 ("Nothing fazes me"):

SCORE: 1—10 _____

Question #12: Can you just say no if something doesn't feel right?

Assign yourself a number between 1 ("I am always getting in over my head") and 10 ("Absolutely"):

SCORE: 1—10 _____

Question #13: Do you believe that you can be pragmatic?

Assign yourself a number between 1 ("There is no room for compromise") and 10 ("A bird in the hand is worth two in the bush"):

SCORE: 1—10 _____

Question #14: Can you set aside and/or delay gratification?

Assign yourself a number between 1 ("As long as I have my car, boat and mansion") and 10 ("I would live in my car to build a business"):

SCORE: 1—10 _____

Question #15: Are you constantly searching for the next get-rich-quick opportunity?

Assign yourself a number between 1 ("This next idea is my ticket to wealth") and 10 ("There is no such thing as a free lunch"):

SCORE: 1—10 _____

Question #16: Would other people call you reliable?

Assign yourself a number between 1 ("Absolutely not") and 10 ("They would want me in their foxhole"):

SCORE: 1—10 _____

Question #17: Are you a good listener?

Assign yourself a number between 1 ("Can you please repeat that again?") and 10 ("I would much rather listen than talk"):

SCORE: 1—10 _____

Question #18: Can you delegate?

Assign yourself a number between 1 ("I might as well just do it myself—again") and 10 ("I've never regretted delegating"):

SCORE: 1—10 _____

Question #19: Can you view your current circumstances in a detached/objective way?

Assign yourself a number between 1 ("I am too emotional to do that") and 10 ("I can look at myself as if I am another person"):

SCORE: 1—10 _____

Question #20: How much exposure have you had to self-employed people?

Assign yourself a number between 1 ("I have never met a self-employed person") and 10 ("Both my parents were self-employed"):

SCORE: 1—10 _____

TOTAL SCORE: _____

~ ~ ~

Below 100: Self-employment is not for you at this time. The good news is that there isn't anything on the quiz that you can't improve upon. It's all going to come down to: "How bad do you want it?"

100–129: You have scored slightly above average in all of the combined traits for measuring your prospects for success. You have a lot of work to do before writing your business plan.

130–149: Your prospects for success are good to very good. Go through the quiz again and pick out the traits where you scored lower and begin to improve in those areas.

150–179: Your prospects for success are outstanding. Let me know about your business venture. I want to invest.

180–200: You obviously didn't read the line before starting the quiz asking you to be "completely honest." Your ego is getting in the way.

~ ~ ~

Just to let you know that I myself am *not* necessarily the "very model" of a modern major self-employed business owner; I took my own quiz and scored a 99. That's a little lower than I would have hoped for, but my prospects for continuing success are at the high end of "good to very good." (If you score between 120–160, your prospects for succeeding are outstanding. So, I have some work to do if I want to make sure that my success continues.)

I scored very well in the areas of execution, judgment, decision-making, flexibility, organization, finances, and integrity. I scored lower on handling failure and adversity and being able to work well under pressure. I also scored lower in the area of sales; I'm a good salesman, but not a great one. I could also stand to be a little less sensitive, more patient, and not quite as emotional when things don't go my way.

Why these questions matter:

#1: Steady paycheck

Many people will not consider self-employment because they live in fear of not having access to a steady paycheck. They believe that entrepreneurs are huge risk takers. But the truth is, most successful entrepreneurs never risk more than they are willing to lose. They carefully plan ahead and grow slowly, learning the ropes of doing business along the way.

Bottom Line: I have interviewed thousands of small business owners. We universally believe that owning your business provides more security than working for someone else. Once you find a winning formula and stick with it, you have much more control over your destiny than having someone else decide your worth or value.

#2: Judgment

Nothing has disappeared from the American landscape during my lifetime faster than good judgment. You can read all the books, including mine, about starting your own business but in the end your success or failure comes down to whether you exercise good or bad judgment. If you exercise good judgment more often than bad, you have a good chance of succeeding. Unfortunately, like experience, good judgment can't be taught. By the time you are in your twenties or thirties, you have either acquired good judgment or you haven't.

Have you exercised good judgment when you've been in charge of your life? Do you demonstrate good judgment in choosing your friends and associates? How about in the jobs you've taken, or in the lifestyle choices you've made? How many times have your business or personal relationships ended in mistrust, or in contempt for the other person or organization? We all have some baggage, but do you have a history of making bad judgment calls or repeating the same mistakes?

On the other hand, if you feel that, by and large, you've been happy with your choices in life, and if you are a person who has generally exercised good judgment, there is a very good chance that you will succeed in business.

Bottom Line: You can read all of the books about self-employment and visit all the websites like this one. But your success or failure in small business will always circle back to whether or not you can exercise good judgment when you need it.

#3: Flexibility

Hopefully, you and your family will only have to make

minimal adjustments to your personal lives when you are starting a small business.

But be aware that there may come a time, even after you have established your business, when you will have to make a significant change in your personal lifestyle to keep your business afloat.

About twenty years ago, when I was publishing my newspaper, one of my advertising clients, a retirement center, suddenly went bankrupt. I had just completed a major printing job for this client. As part of my agreement with the printers who handled the job, I had promised to pay them once the client paid me. When the client went out of business, I got stuck with a printing bill for $10,000.

To keep my business from going under, I had to move out of my four-bedroom house and into a condo that I had originally leased to use as office space. This move saved me about $38,000 a year, and enabled me to pay off my debt to the printers. I'm glad to report that I have since been able to move back into a four-bedroom house.

What happened to me was an extreme case. I was single at the time, so changing my address, while certainly a great inconvenience, was easier for me than it would have been if I had been married with a family. Hopefully, you will never be forced to give up your house to save your business. But the more flexible you can be in adjusting your personal lifestyle to suit your business, the more that lifestyle will be an asset to you instead of a burden.

Flexibility is a required trait for running a business. You will make lifestyle decisions and changes based on how well your business is doing. Talk with your family about how your business will affect them, because it will. Make sure they support your efforts. You may have to trade in the brand new SUV for a used car—or skip that vacation to the Caribbean this year.

Bottom Line: Your prospects for success will increase enormously if you and your family can make lifestyle adjustments as needed.

#4: Organization

In real estate, the motto is location, "Location, location, location." In business, it's "Organization organization, organization."

Time is your precious commodity. The best use of your time should be spent selling. Contract out repetitive functions like bookkeeping.

Also, think about this: Saving two hours commute time a day will save you one full year of productivity in approximately ten years.

Organization, or lack thereof, often makes the difference between success and failure in the business. Success in business is all about developing systems that make doing your job and its various tasks easier and more profitable with each passing day. Time is money. And the more organized you are, the faster and easier it will be for you to manage your business and make money.

Organization means opening your daily mail and or e-mail and deciding what to do with your inputs on the spot, instead of letting it stack up. It means returning important phone calls or e-mails within twenty-four hours. It means having a filing system for bills, invoices, receipts, tax records, etc., so you can locate whatever document you need quickly. It means having a business card of your own that you can hand out to people— with your company name, address, phone, e-mail address, and website URL—so they can contact you easily. It means making sure that your car is in working order, so you won't miss important appointments. The more organized you are, the more you can accomplish in a day, a week, or a year.

When you hear that someone is "burned out" from running their own business, it usually means that the business owner is exhausted from the daily effort of trying to run a disorganized business. A business owner who is disorganized is continuously flailing away like the worst government bureaucrats or people who work for large organizations. These people can afford to be disorganized because their salary is not based on organizational ability. For the self-employed business owner, organizational ability is an essential survival tool. I firmly believe that being organized is one of the major reasons I am still in business today.

Being organized also instills a sense of confidence in your clients and potential clients, while not being organized tends to have the opposite effect. There used to be a print shop across the street from my office. I say "used to be" because it has since gone out of business. I suspect the main reason this print shop went out of business was a lack of organization among its employees.

Each time I visited the print shop, I saw empty and unplugged computers, diskettes stacked everywhere, and papers and files spread out across the desks and piled on the floor behind the counters. The entire shop had a look of general chaos.

After a time, I stopped using this print shop for large projects where I had to leave an original set of documents with them. I was afraid that would misplace or lose my documents. I often wondered how many customers they lost because of their poor organizational skills.

Riding in someone's vehicle tells me a lot about whether or not I want to work with them on a professional basis. If the car is relatively clean on the outside, and if the inside is not littered with fast-food wrappers and old newspapers, it tells me that this person is organized and pays attention to detail. If someone is organized enough to make sure that their car is presentable, I imagine that their home and office are probably also organized as well. If I conduct business with this person, my project with them will probably be completed in an orderly manner.

Bottom Line: Always be thinking of ways of making your company more efficient.

#5: Decisiveness

Bruce Nordstrom, former CEO of Nordstrom, Inc., taught me a valuable lesson in business long before I even considered going into business for myself. In the late 1970s, Mr. Nordstrom served as a volunteer and advisor on a task force that was seeking a transit solution for downtown Seattle. At the time, I was the Public Affairs Director for the project. I was providing staff support for this task force. I noticed some significant things about the way that Mr. Nordstrom communicated with other people.

First, when he was in his office, Mr. Nordstrom never used an administrative assistant or secretary to screen his calls. He always answered the phone in person. If I called to ask if he would consider chairing a new transportation committee or if he would do an interview with a Seattle newspaper about the challenges of transportation facing our region, he wouldn't keep me waiting for my answer. He never said to me, "Well, I don't know. Why don't you call me next week, and I'll let you know if I can do it."

After I made my pitch, he would pause for about five seconds and give me his answer. "No, I can't chair that task force at this time." Or, "Yes I can do the interview. Set it up for this time next week." Our conversations generally lasted thirty seconds or less. He didn't waste his time or mine floundering about. He knew instantly whether he had the time, knowledge, or desire to proceed with my request. When he was asked a question he acted decisively.

Bottom Line: This is a great lesson, and one that is imperative if you wish to start a successful business. With each successful project, you establish a new standard for future expectations.

#6: Execution

Thomas Edison said, "Genius is one percent inspiration, ninety-nine percent perspiration."[2] In other words, an idea means nothing unless it's executed. Proper execution is the driving force behind success. I've seen very creative minds come up with some great ideas but when it comes to putting the ideas into action—no one's home.

By the time he invented the light bulb, Thomas Edison was already famous for having invented a number of other useful devices, including the phonograph. With the backing of investors like J. P. Morgan, Edison set out to invent an incandescent lamp that would run on electrical power. After

---

[2] Spoken statement (c. 1903); published in *Harper's Monthly*, September, 1932

Edison created his initial design for the light bulb, he assembled a team of scientists and electrical engineers to help him in his laboratory in Menlo Park, New Jersey.

The first step was to have a glass blower blow a glass bulb that could be used as the basis for the lamp. For each experiment, Edison would insert a filament wire inside the bulb, then seal the bulb and vacuum the air out of it. His engineers would then hook the bulb up to a portable generator, turn on the electrical power, and hope for the best. Usually, either the filament wire would burn out in only a few seconds or the glass bulb would burst, and Edison and his team would have to go back to the drawing board.

It took Edison and his men over a year of experimentation to find a filament wire that would conduct electricity long enough to be practical. For a long time, they experimented with platinum wires rolled in carbon, but these only burned for a few minutes. Then Edison made a carbonized strip of cardboard in the shape of a horseshoe, and put that inside the bulb, and it burned for about forty hours. Then he and his men experimented with wires made from various types of Japanese bamboo, and these burned even longer.

Finally, a few years after he had patented the light bulb in 1881, Edison discovered that tungsten wires could burn for over 1,000 hours inside a light bulb. He had perfected his product, as he said, through "ninety-nine percent perspiration," and tungsten wires are still used in light bulbs today.

I have met many great thinkers, talkers, and planners, but very few people who could successfully execute their ideas on a consistent basis.

One person who has influenced me a great deal is the late author Jackie Collins, even though I have never read any of her books. I once saw her interviewed on a television talk show, in which she spoke about her book, *Hollywood Housewives.* After her book became a best seller, she said, people would come up to her at dinner parties or book signings, and say, "Oh, that was my book! I could have written that book! You took my ideas! I should have written that book!"

Ms. Collins said that she soon got very tired of hearing this. She resented the idea that other people thought that this should have been "their" book. She wanted to say to them, "No, this is not your book! This is my book! I was the one who got up at 4 a.m. every day, and worked fourteen-hour days for six months researching, writing, editing, and getting this book published."

I have never forgotten this interview with Jackie Collins. Her point is that an idea means absolutely nothing unless it is executed. An idea or concept will remain a dream unless you are willing to put in the long hours necessary to make your dream a reality.

Execution is an absolute must for sustaining a business. As mundane as it sounds, execution is what keeps the business going. Jackie Collins wrote many bestsellers. If *Hollywood Housewives* had been her only book, she would have been long forgotten by now. Her book made *The New York Times* best seller's list because she had the talent to write a compelling book that could reach a wide audience. But her work ethics and her consistency in writing more books have kept her on this list.

Again, it's the same with business. If you have the initiative to start a business that delivers a useful product or service to your clients, they will remember that product or service. But if you keep delivering that useful product or service to your clients, they will always come back to you for more.

Bottom Line: You will succeed only if you can take your inspiration and turn it into reality.

#7: Sales

When I talk with other people about self-employment, the thought of "selling" is where most people seem to struggle. They give me a "deer in the headlights" look or "I can't sell" glance. If you don't want to—or more importantly won't—sell, running a business is not for you. As a small business owner, selling your product or service is where you should be spending the bulk of your time.

No matter what size the company, you are the CEO. In reality CEO equals COS: Chief of Sales. Your primary function will always be to sell your product or service. No one else can represent your business the way you can. Don't abdicate that responsibility to someone else, at least not in the beginning.

No matter how high-tech we become, sales is still a contact sport. It's about developing and nurturing relationships with existing and potential clients. People buy from people, not from technology. The best salespeople view themselves as consultants rather than salespeople. This is an important mindset. Obviously, your product or service is of value or you wouldn't be offering it to them.

I once had a potential client that I absolutely knew would benefit from advertising in my newspaper, and later on my radio show. I never harassed them, but I would check in with them every six months or so, to see if they were ready to come on board. Finally, after eight years, the client had a new directive from the home office to achieve more local exposure. My radio show became a perfect vehicle for them. (When you hear the phrase "Patience is for losers," don't believe it.)

As Chief of Sales, your goal should be to position yourself as the expert in your field. No one should even consider going to someone else. In my case, I promote Casey Communications Inc. as the leading expert in radio. No agency in the United States can create, secure, and execute radio programming better than Casey Communications Inc.

Buying a home is probably the largest investment that anyone will ever make in their lifetime. But when it comes to selling homes, many real estate brokers have the sales mentality of a door-to-door vacuum salesman. Once the transaction is completed, the client never hears from their realtor again. In fact, this is where the relationship should just be beginning. The average family in the United States moves every five to seven years. Most family moves are made within the same community.

If you are a real estate broker, you will have an edge over your competition if you think of the home buyer as a client rather than a someone just buying a house. You should position yourself as the expert consultant in all matters of residential real estate. If a client wants to know how much their home has appreciated, they should call you first.

Bottom Line: The pathway to becoming a successful real estate broker is exactly the type of mentality you should develop, no matter what business you choose. If you believe in what you are doing—you are not selling—you're informing.

#8: Ethics

For the self-employed, the most important decision you will make is the people you are surrounded by within your business. This includes people that you hire and clients that you pursue. Are they honest and straightforward? If they make a promise, do they keep it? If they make a commitment, do they stick to it? Pay close attention to how your clients and associates deal with people on a personal level. How do they treat a waiter at a restaurant?

I have made my share of mistakes in business, but I have

always made a point of adhering to ethics and integrity. If a client overpays me by even just a dollar, my accountant is under strict instructions to return the money. If I give you my word, nothing will stop me from trying to fulfill that commitment. If I fail, I will apologize and take full responsibility for my shortcomings.

What about you? Do you hold to your word? You may be able to hide from ethics if you work in a large company, but when you are a self-employed business owner, there is nowhere to hide: there is only you and your word.

Bottom Line: Surrounding yourself with ethical people is money in the bank.

#9: Multitasking

Just because you are a great artist doesn't mean that you can sell your artwork. Just because you can cook a great steak does not mean that you can run a restaurant. If you decide to open a restaurant, the quality of your food is only one aspect of successfully sustaining a restaurant. (It is a very important aspect, but just one of the many reasons that will determine whether you will succeed as a restaurant owner or not.)

You must possess core competencies in finance, marketing, hiring, managing, organization, sales, décor selection, leadership, execution, problem solving, option thinking, being accountable, pragmatic, ethics, and have a great eye for picking a suitable location.

I know an artist who is quite talented. A couple of very famous people have purchased his paintings. He participates in popular art shows in the United States and England. I have a feeling you will be hearing his name some day, and that's not just because he is a talented artist. He is very disciplined and possesses many of the core competencies that I listed above.

I visited him once in his studio, in the basement of his home. I asked him how he did it? He said it's like any other job. "I have to paint every night, even if I don't feel like it." He works between 10 p.m. and 3 a.m., seven days a week. He said that the creative part of what he does is just part of the process. He said that his rigorous schedule is what separates him from the competition.

You can be the most creative person in the world or have the best idea this side of the Mississippi, but unless you can multitask, your enterprise will go nowhere. I often think that successful entrepreneurs would make great jugglers in a circus.

Bottom Line: The most successful entrepreneurs are good at many things rather than great at just a few things. They can multitask on many different fronts.

#10: Finances

Can you balance your checkbook? Do you have a savings account? Do you know how to manage your credit cards? Or are you always behind on your payments? Your ability to manage personal finances has everything to do with your success or failure as a small business owner.

If you don't bring in more money than you spend—you will fail. Brilliant observation, right? It seems obvious but how many millions of small businesses failed because the owner is neither financially competent or disciplined.

I was hosting my radio show on small business success and a caller called in with the idea of starting an educational center that targeted young adults. The concept sounded viable, and it certainly filled a niche. I asked about finances, and she said that she was too far in debt to use any of her own money. I stopped her right there. Our conversation was over as far as I was concerned. If you don't have a handle on your personal finances, you have no business going into business.

I believe that you should be in a position to invest at least 25 percent of your personal income (preferably more) into your startup operation. Scale your startup business to what you can afford. Avoid borrowing money from investors as much as possible. (If you want to tutor children, perhaps you could start your business out of your home or apartment.) I can absolutely guarantee that if your own money is invested in this game, you will watch the bottom line a lot closer.

In my first ten years in business, I drove a used car with no monthly payments. I was also successful in negotiating free office space. It was a rat hole of a space, but it was free. Since there is truly no free lunch, the condition for the free office space was that I had to print my newspaper at that particular publishing house. I later calculated that by driving a used car and negotiating free office space, I saved my company over $400,000 in a ten-year period. That is real money.

The decisions you make prior to even writing your business plan will dictate whether or not you will succeed in the long run. For example, you might ask yourself: Should I go into business with a partner?

What happens when you take on a partner? You have just cut your income potential in half. I am not suggesting that you shouldn't consider a partner under any circumstances. But I also suggest that you really examine your motives. Is it because you don't have the confidence to run your business yourself? Is it because you don't like to sell? (See test question on selling.) These are not valid reasons to bring on a partner. Real entrepreneurs don't need partners. (Mentors and free agents, yes! But partners, no.)

Bottom Line: If you haven't been fiscally disciplined in your personal life, how can you expect to be fiscally disciplined when it comes to sustaining your business? Don't even think about starting your own business until you have paid off your credit cards and developed a healthy savings account.

#11: Adversity

Are you able to keep going when things go bad, not just in business, but in your personal life as well? Do you have the emotional capacity to handle a personal trauma and run a business at the same time? In one period of about four years, I lost both of my parents and a brother. At times, it was hard for me to stay focused and keep my business going through all of that adversity, but somehow I made it through. Unfortunately, this is one of those personality traits that you can't really measure until it happens to you.

If you have been through an emotional crisis before, and you were able to find the strength to keep going in the face of adversity, it will be an advantage to your business if and when another such crisis hits. If you tend to become unraveled for an extended period of time during an emotional crisis, it doesn't mean you shouldn't go into business for yourself. But you should be aware of your own emotional limitations and how they can affect your business.

Bottom Line: Your ability to handle emotional challenges will be a factor in sustaining your business. Your prospects for success will be much higher if you can endure during times of difficulty.

#12: Saying "No"

Learning to say "No" is an essential skill for the self-employed. First, never make a financial decision on the spot. Second, if you're not interested, let the solicitor know immediately. You're actually doing them a favor. Third, plan out the cash outlays you will need in advance, and stick to the plan.

In business, you have to make tough calls. I believe that many people don't go into business for themselves because they have a problem with saying the word "No." To succeed in business, you must be firm and direct. This means you must know when to turn someone down.

Some No's are easy, such as when you get a call asking if you'd like to change your long-distance service. Unless you are one of those rare people in the world who is actually looking for a better long-distance service, simply say "Thank you. I'm not interested" and hang up. If you are offered a scheme that promises to make $100,000 in six months, you would be smart to turn it down. Again, if it seems too good to be true, it probably is.

Other No's may be a bit more difficult. If you sense that a client is a "Taker," or that they will be difficult to work with, or that something about them is not quite honest, it can be very hard to turn them down, especially if you need the business. If you sense that the client does not really need your services, it can be hard to refuse them if you know that working with them would be very profitable.

But it is better to be honest than to lead them on the business equivalent of a wild goose chase, making them spend money for business services that they don't really need. They will respect you more if you tell them the truth, and they will almost always come back to you when the time comes that they really do need your services.

If you are someone who has a problem with saying "No." you might want to reconsider going into business for yourself. Saying "No" is being tough when you have to be.

Bottom Line: Don't make it hard for your customers to contact you by forcing them to use pagers, Facebook, texting, or complicated voicemail systems, just because you want to avoid solicitations. Just learn to say, "No thank you," to any solicitations, and you will be fine.

#13: Pragmatism

American Heritage Dictionary—Pragmatic: concerned with facts or actual occurrences.[3] *"Just the facts, ma'am."*[4] If you remember the television show Dragnet, you will remember that signature line. Sergeant Joe Friday repeated it when he was trying to extract information from a witness to a crime. Sergeant Friday was always trying to get the witness to focus on the facts.

I like a phrase that was said about Dr. Martin Luther King Jr.: "He had dreams but he was not a dreamer."[5] He dreamed of equal rights for all Americans. He dreamed that one day

---

[3] William Morris, *The American Heritage Dictionary* (Boston: Houghton Mifflin, 1982).

[4] Jack Webb, writer, *Dragnet*, NBC.

[5] *A TV spot celebrating Martin Luther King Jr.'s birthday*, 1995.

there would be an African-American President. He also knew that in order to reach those goals, it would require smaller steps. He was pragmatic.

In 1956, the Montgomery, Alabama Transit System, by law required African-Americans to ride in the back of the bus. On one December day Rosa Parks, an African-American woman, refused to give up her seat to a white man. She was arrested. Dr. King led a boycott of the Montgomery Transit System that lasted for a year. The boycott almost destroyed the Montgomery Transit System financially. The law was repealed.

This was a very pragmatic first step for the Civil Rights movement. It was also a very pragmatic decision on the part of the Montgomery Transit System. They didn't change the law because they thought that it was immoral. They changed the law because it saved the transit agency from bankruptcy.

What do these examples have to do with sustaining a business? Everything. You may want to occupy that signature downtown office space, but it just isn't very practical right now. Your aunt may tell you that you are a talented guitar player, but supporting yourself in that profession isn't very practical. The facts just don't support it.

There are too many romantics going into business for themselves. They have a cool concept but don't know if there is a market to support their product or service. This is understandable. The people who reach hero status in this country are the ones who appear to have risked it all and are now living on Park Avenue in Manhattan. This will never work for 99 percent of rest of us but that fact is ignored.

Bottom Line: Inc. Magazine had a cover story that said "...the smartest entrepreneurs are satisfying needs, not wants." If you want to increase your prospects for small business success, be pragmatic: 1) Find a niche, and 2) Solve someone's problem.

#14: Gratification

There has never been a better time in history to go into business for yourself than right now. (I know the economy is terrible in many places but there are also many opportunities.) We have resources available to help us launch our business that our parents or grandparents never dreamed of. Unprecedented access to technology, financing, education, health care, personal wealth, knowledge, and mobility are all at higher levels than ever before.

However, there is a downside to all these advantages. We have created a culture of Instant Gratification, in which we feel we must have it all right here, right now. At times, it seems as if our lives are ruled by speed. This is a culture of instant customer service, overnight shoes, twitter, texting, thirty-minute oil changes and so on.

Thanks to the technological advancements of the past fifty years, almost anything we could ever need is a remote control or mouse click or app away. We can download books in less than one minute.

Instant gratification and starting your own business do not mix. It takes time, typically three to five years to build a sustainable business. During that time, you must live frugally, save as much money as you can and keep out of as debt as much as possible. It will serve you and your business well if you can replace the creed of Instant Gratification in your mind with an ethic of sensible decision-making and with a lot of patience.

I believe the biggest reason why many people will not go into business for themselves is that they are unwilling to make the necessary sacrifices to make it happen. When you talk to would-be entrepreneurs, they say all the right things about wanting to start their own business. But when you probe further, many times you find out that what is really important to them is having a five-bedroom home with a three car garage and a band new SUV.

We must make choices in our lives. If you want a top-paying corporate job, you might have to surrender control of your time. You will give up some independence and perhaps some freedom of thought and association.

But in exchange, you will acquire a nice house in a nice neighborhood and plenty of toys. Again, there is nothing wrong with this kind of life. If that is your choice of how you want to live, I wish you well.

But if you really have the desire to start your own business, it can be done.

And yes, if you stick with your business long enough, you will be able to eventually purchase a five-bedroom home with three-car-garage if that is what you want.

Just not now.

Bottom Line: If you can put off that swimming pool or brand new SUV because sustaining your business is more important than any luxury item, your prospects for small business success are much greater. Understand that when you are a self-employed, your business will always come first. It will be the primary motivation behind most of your major lifestyle decisions. If you define success on how may toys you have in the garage, you will have a hard time sustaining your business.

#15: Getting rich

I'm sure you've been exposed to many "Get Rich Quick" opportunities. The promise of instant wealth can be seductive. The only people who usually get rich from these quick money schemes are the ones who offer them. Your goal should be to build a business that will last a lifetime. It may take ten or even twenty years. But your business could be the source of better financial security than your day job ever could have possibly been. Your mindset should not be geared toward making fast money but toward establishing a long-term business that will provide security for you when things go bad.

Bottom Line: Your odds for instant wealth are higher in Las Vegas.

Question #16: Reliability

The world is made up of reliable and unreliable people. It's essential to surround yourself with reliable people. This includes your customers. Also, keep an eye out for the "one-day wonders." They may design a great website, but won't be around to manage it. As with everything, no one is 100-percent reliable or 100-percent unreliable. Succeeding in business will be so much easier if your efforts are supported by reliable people—or in other words, by people who show up.

As a business owner, you will quickly learn to distinguish the reliable associates from the unreliable ones. The reliable associates are those who always show up when you ask them to, and who deliver what you need from them time and again. The unreliable ones are those who show up late for meetings, miss deadlines, and turn in substandard work. The more you surround yourself with reliable people, the more your business will prosper. Of course, this assumes that you are a reliable person, and that you always complete your projects, turn in your best effort, show up for meetings on time, etc.

Bottom Line: This may be a bit dramatic, but here's a good question to ask when bringing someone into your business: "If my life were on the line, would I want this person in my foxhole?"

#17: Listening

The ability to take the time to listen and actually absorb what is going on is a skill that is severely lacking today. I sometimes refer to this skill as the ability to "read a room." With 24-hour cable stations, blogging, tweeting, emailing, Facebooking, texting, etc., there is little time left to just listen. If you don't get your point across in fifteen seconds or less, the eyes of the person you are talking to will often begin to glaze over. (Maybe it's that I just need to shorten and spice up my stories. That's possible too.)

You can pick up valuable information on what a potential client or customer is looking for if you just listen to what they are telling you. Many times a small business owner (myself included) will go into a client meeting with a preconceived notion of what we think the client needs—and that, of course, is our product or service. After all, we've created this wonderful product or service that they just can't live without.

I became better at making sales when I learned to use my first meeting with a potential client as an opportunity for them to tell me everything about their business. I've developed the mindset that, in my first meeting with a client, I am a reporter covering a story. I let the potential client talk, while I listen to them and write down as much information as I can. At the end of the meeting, I take a few minutes to summarize their major points.

I don't try to sell them anything during our first encounter unless it's obvious that they need my service. Otherwise, I take what I've learned from the client during our first meeting, and get back to them in day or two with a well-thought out proposal. This demonstrates to my client that I am carefully considering their needs and how to meet them.

Bottom Line: Being a good listener is one of the most important ingredient for becoming a successful business owner. You can pick up valuable information on what a potential client or customer is looking for if you just take time to listen to what they are telling you.

#18: Delegating

Do you trust people? I ask this because it will have an enormous impact on your business. A big challenge facing small business owners is that we don't delegate enough. This is understandable. We went into business in the first place because we wanted more control of our lives. We have difficulty letting go and a tendency to control other people.

Learn how to delegate the small tasks and your business will run a lot smoother. You shouldn't try to micro-manage. If a person is not performing, find someone else who can give you the results you need. If you can't delegate, it means ...

You are a lousy manager. You don't trust people. You can't communicate well with people, and therefore ... you won't succeed in business.

If you can't delegate, you will burn out sooner or later. I believe that a lack of organizational skills is the number one reason why business owners "burn out." Not being able to delegate tasks is a close second. When you first start your business, you have a lot of extra energy because everything is so new. But eventually the novelty wears off. As your business grows, you will soon find that you can't handle every task on every project all by yourself. It will be better if you have some qualified contract workers or employees on hand to pick up the slack and take care of some of the more mundane tasks.

When I put together a radio ad campaign, almost all of the actual production work will be done by free agents or contract workers. Once the client and I have determined the main concepts for the campaign, I call up one of my agents, a writer, and give them the concepts for the radio spots. At that point, my job is basically finished. The writer writes the radio spots and sends them on to another free agent, the producer. The producer produces the spots (with the help of other free agents to handle recording, voice-overs, and sound effects), and sends them back to the client for approval. If the client approves, another free agent then distributes the radio spots to a station. The producer then calls me to let me know that the project is complete.

Some people who have observed my business think that I should be more "in charge," that I should supervise more or actually be on hand when my free agents perform their duties. I prefer to treat people as professionals, and to give my free agents plenty of room to succeed or to fail. But more important, I make them totally accountable for their part in the process. If something goes wrong, I will know exactly where the problem is and I can deal with it on the spot. If people do not execute their tasks properly, I will replace them.

Like me, my free agents must be accessible. One requirement I have for all my free agents is that they must provide me with backup if they are not accessible for any reason. I don't care if the free agent who produces my radio spots goes on a six-month vacation to Australia, as long as he makes arrangements for a competent backup producer who to take his place that will fully execute his tasks while he is gone. The burden is on my producer to make sure that there is no fall-off in the radio production area of my business. That goes for all of the free agents who work with me.

I provide most of my free agents with direct access to my clients. I monitor the contacts very closely, and I am always asking the client if they enjoy working with this or that free agent. If the response is yes, I probe further. I ask again if they really feel that way, or if they are just trying to be cordial. I make it very clear that they should call me immediately if they are not 100-percent satisfied with the free agent's performance. Since I make sure that the people I work with are not only very competent but also have pleasant personalities, it is usually not a problem for my agents to contact my clients.

I have worked with too many people who over-supervise or micro-manage. Another term to describe these kinds of people is "control freaks." They want to be involved in every detail of every project. They stifle the creativity of the people who work for them. Even more damaging, they slow down the process of getting the job done. This is not only annoying, it also hurts productivity. With control over every detail, it is impossible to determine who is really responsible for what aspect of the project. This type of management style may work (barely) in a corporate structure, but it won't work if you are trying to sustain your own business.

Bottom Line: Learn how to delegate small tasks, and your business will run a lot smoother. At the same time, you shouldn't try to micro-manage. If a person is not performing, find someone else who can give you the results you need.

#19: Detachment

Touching the Void is a movie based on a true story, about two climbers who become separated in bad weather while mountain climbing in Peru. One of the climbers breaks his leg and his prospect for surviving looks highly unlikely. But when this climber was at his lowest point, he somehow found clarity by viewing his predicament in a detached, more objective way. He was less emotional and more focused on finding a way out of his situation, which he eventually did.

The ability to look at your business through the eyes of your customer is an essential trait for success. Emotions always come into play when running your business, but if you can step back and look at your current challenge in an objective manner, your prospects for success will be much higher.

Bottom Line: The more you can view your business and life experiences as an impartial observer, the higher your prospects for success.

#20: Exposure

This is the only question on the test that is black and white. You have absolutely no control on the outcome. You either grew up around someone (i.e., parents, older brother/sister etc.) who were self-employed or you didn't. I didn't. My father was a salesman for medium sized company and my mother a homemaker.

This question is very important. If you were exposed to someone close to you who had built a business, you have first hand knowledge of what it takes to sustain a business. You are in a much stronger position to make an informed decision on whether self-employment is something that you want to pursue. You know the late nights, the vacations cut short or canceled because your father/mother had to pay attention to the business. You may have even pitched in to help in the family business from time to time.

If you were exposed to a small business, your decision whether you want to take this step is based on reality. Getting as close to reality as you can is always a good thing.

Bottom Line: I know many people who want absolutely nothing to do with running a small business because they grew up in a family business. There are just as many people who see self-employment as their only option based on observing a small business. If you are one of these people, you have an enormous advantage over the rest of us. Your prospects for success are very high should you decide to take the step into self-employment. You should give yourself an extra ten points on the test.

THE 5 REASONS FOR
SELF-EMPLOYMENT

L et's explore some of the reasons why self-employment might be a good option for you.

You don't need this book to tell you we live in an age of erratic business cycles and volatile market trends. Corporate employment no longer provides the same level of security or the same promise of success that it once did. It seems as if every day we hear a new report on the latest victims of Corporate America's declining business practices. Executives and stockholders now determine the fates of employees based not on the individual employee's value or job performance, but on the company's profits and losses.

Workers lose their jobs, savings, and pensions to poor corporate leadership. In extreme cases, major corporations with thousands of employees have incurred huge scandals or have even been forced out of business by the poor decision-making, reckless greed, and fraudulent business practices of their executives. Even in this unstable business climate, many people still think they have no choice but to keep working for someone else. Others who have managed to keep their jobs in spite of hard times are still quite satisfied with corporate employment.

But some people dream of being self-employed, of owning their own independent businesses. They want to break away from the boss, the company, or the industry where they seem to be stuck in perpetual servitude. They want to escape the "rat race" of corporate employment and take control of their own destinies. They don't want someone else telling them how much money they're worth, what time they should come to work, when they can take vacations, eat lunch, take a break, etc., And those of us who are already self-employed hope to stay in business long enough to see the fruits of our labor.

If you're reading this book, you probably have a strong desire for the independence of self-employment. Again, the purpose of this book is to give you an accurate sense of your prospects for success as an entrepreneur.

~

This book identifies the critical personality traits for self-employment

~

If you do join the ranks of the self-employed, rest assured you won't be alone. The number of self-employed workers and free agents in the American workforce is growing so rapidly that no one is quite sure how many there are or will be in the near future.

According to *Forbes* magazine, as of 2014[6]:

❑ There are 28 million small businesses in the US.

❑ Over 50% of the American workforce is employed by a small business.

❑ 52% of small businesses are home-based.

In addition, there's a growing section of the workforce known variously as "soloists," "freelancers," or "independent professionals" who have no single employer and who regularly move from job to job, from contract to contract. Pew Research Center, American "fact tank" based in Washington, D.C., counted 44 million people in this category in 2014, or roughly one-third of the American workforce.[7] Clearly, anyone who

---

[6] Jason Nazar, "16 Surprising Statistics About Small Businesses," *Forbes*, September 9, 2013, http://www.forbes.com/sites/jasonnazar/2013/09/09/16-surprising-statistics-about-small-businesses/#5f3f01653078.

[7] Kochhar, Rakesh. 2015. "Three-in-Ten U.S. Jobs Are Held by the Self-Employed and the Workers They Hire: Hiring More

wishes to become self-employed will find him or herself in good company.

What is security anyway?

For many people, self-employment is simply not an option, because they think it's too big a risk. Many people feel more comfortable with a 40-hour-per-week job and the security of a steady paycheck. This is understandable. The prospect of living on a park bench can be daunting.

~

**Most successful entrepreneurs
are not huge risk takers**

~

We never risk more than we are willing to lose. We know when to walk away from the blackjack table. We keep enough money in our savings account to live on for at least a year. If things don't work out, we always have a fallback position.

Successful entrepreneurs develop a solid plan of attack (often referred to as a business plan). We keep our overhead low and grow slowly. We're not just trying out self-

---

Prevalent Among Self-Employed Asians, Whites and Men."
Washington, D.C.: Pew Research Center, October.

employment to see if it works. We've made a commitment to the entrepreneurial lifestyle. Most entrepreneurs are of the mindset that the security of a paycheck or security in life are illusions. You can do things to put yourself in a more secure position, but none of us knows exactly what tomorrow will bring.

I've interviewed hundreds of small business owners. We universally believe that owning your own business provides more security than working for someone else. Once you find a winning formula and stick with it, you have much more control over your destiny than you do when you let a business executive, supervisor, or manager decide your worth or value.

Why go into business?

The most basic step of self-employment—deciding to start a business—is not as simple as it seems. It's easy to say, "Okay, I'll just start my own business," quit your job, and plunge right in. Easy, but very foolish! Before you decide to become an entrepreneur, answer this question: "Why do I want to start my own business?"

I firmly believe you must have some deep and very strong reasons for wanting to be self-employed. Only you can say for yourself what those reasons are. Hopefully, you're starting a business for the right reasons:

Good Reason: I want to control my own destiny, both intellectually and financially.

Bad Reason: I'm tired of wearing a suit and tie to work. I want to be able to work at home in Bermuda shorts.

Good Reason: I have the experience that it will take to turn this concept into a profitable and successful business.

Bad Reason: My grandmother told me that I make a great meatloaf, so I think I'll open up a restaurant.

Good Reason: I want to slowly build a small business that will provide long-term security for myself and my family; a business that will keep going even through the hard times.

Bad reason: I want to cash in on the latest Internet/high-tech fad, create my own company, and make a million dollars.

It's all about execution

Having a dream is a very small part on the road to success. Execution of your dream is the driving force to success.

~

Thomas Edison said, "Vision without execution is just hallucination."[8]

---

[8] Bryan Stolle, "Vision Without Execution Is Just Hallucination," *Forbes*, July 22, 2014, http://www.forbes.com/sites/bryanstolle/2014/07/22/vision-without-execution-is-just-hallucination/#31df6f6b3bee.

~

Self-employment is all about developing and executing business systems that work over the long run. It's about getting cash, so it can flow. It's about paying your vendors on time and making sure you are square with the tax man. It's about paying your rent, meeting deadlines, and juggling numerous tasks at once. It's about keeping your overhead low and staying out of debt. (As dull as it sounds, Apple and Microsoft will only survive if they bring in more dollars at the end of the year than they spend. This is a basic goal for any business, but how often is this goal violated or not met?)

There was a day not long ago when people went into business for all the right reasons. Usually, it was because they had ideas or dreams they wanted to build into successful, long-term enterprises. They may have had original business concepts or brilliant discoveries that the world had never seen before. Or their businesses might have been more ordinary, like farms, barbershops, retail stores, dry-cleaning services, visiting maid services, or engineering firms. These businesses were nothing mind-boggling, but they did provide the entrepreneur with more freedom, more money, and more time. It wasn't about IPOs or how much money your company could return on investment to stockholders. It was called true capitalism.

My five reasons for self-employment

It's very important to believe in yourself and your product or service if you want your business to be successful in the long run. If you are just "in it for the money," it will be much harder to succeed. As a self-employed business owner, you will go through many highs and lows both financially and emotionally. Your ultimate goal is to have the highs not so high and the lows not too low. You want to achieve consistency.

Having strong reasons for starting your own business will help you to get through the difficult times. When I wasn't making a steady income, it helped that I believed strongly in what I was doing. Below is a list of my primary reasons for starting my own business. As a marketing and communications specialist, the clients that I serve and the type of work that I do have changed dramatically over the last 25-plus years. What never changed are my basic reasons for wanting my own business.

Here are the reasons why I, Paul E. Casey, want to own my own business:

Reason #1: I want to develop a successful communications business. As part of my business, I want to employ a creative and extremely competent communications team made up of free agents.

Over twenty-five years ago, I created my own independent communications firm, Casey Communications Inc., located in Seattle. What started out as a small publishing firm has evolved into a successful media buying business. I specialize in buying airtime for clients who wish to advertise on the radio, television, and increasingly on social media.

This first reason is the most crucial of the five. It explains in a nutshell what my business is and what my overall goals are for the business itself. I believe that everyone who wishes to start his or her own business should have a similar "first reason." In other words, your "first reason" for wanting to go into business for yourself should be a clear and specific definition of the kind of business you want to create.

Reason #2: I want freedom of time.

I'm in the process of achieving freedom of time. Like many goals in life, freedom of time is something that you must work for continuously. To me, freedom of time means spending as much time as possible doing the things I enjoy, whether it's owning and operating my own business, spending time with my family and friends, or hacking my afternoon away on the golf course. (I get it that people who don't play golf wonder why in the hell you would spend money chasing after a white ball. I often wonder about that myself.)

As a self-employed business owner, I strive to be the master of my own work schedule. I can set my own pace and schedule the time to get my work done as I see fit. This doesn't mean, of course, that I can sit back and relax in my office every day. Running a business always takes a great deal of effort. But I don't have anyone else telling me that I have to clock in by 8, have lunch from 12 to 1, and clock out at 5.

Freedom of time also means I'm free to travel whenever I want to. One reason I went into the communications business was that I knew it would give me opportunities to travel while still conducting business. If I had opened a small retail store that required my presence every day, traveling would have been a lot more difficult.

Reason #3: I want freedom of expression and association.

It's very important for me to be able to express my opinions without fear of repercussions. We live in a country where freedom of speech is a cherished right. Freedom of expression is more important to me than money. I'm not suggesting that I'm free to express any opinion I have whenever I want to, but I'm closer to that goal today than ever before.

I'm also achieving freedom of association. As a self-employed business owner, I have the freedom to seek out my own clients. I also have the freedom to refuse to work with clients that I don't want to work with. If I sense that certain clients are not quite ethical in their business practices, if I don't like their attitudes (e.g., they try to talk me down on my fee), or if I don't feel they really need my services (perhaps their businesses are not yet ready for radio advertising), I have the freedom to turn them down. Also, I don't have to work for a lousy or incompetent supervisor or manager. Life is too short.

Reason #4: Using the latest communications technology, I want to create a virtual office that will allow me to conduct my business anytime, anywhere.

I have created my own virtual office that enables me to conduct my business anytime, anywhere.

When I travel, I check emails, text messages, and voicemails twice a day. I don't anticipate having to work more than thirty minutes on any given day. Thanks to my virtual office, I've been able to take over two months of vacation this year. While I'm away from the physical office, my business will continue to run via an assortment of free agents. I have enough confidence in these agents to know they will keep things running smoothly in my absence.

When I tell people who work 9-to-5 jobs that I'm taking my smartphone and laptop with me to Hawaii, they think I'm a workaholic who can't get away from his business. But when they go on their annual two- to three-week vacations, they are generally so burned out that they want nothing to do with their companies or professions.

Because I enjoy what I do, it doesn't cause me undue stress to keep in touch with my business clients while I'm on the road. Having a virtual office enables me to check in with my clients and my free agents to make sure that things are running smoothly in my absence.

Reason #5: I want to achieve financial independence.

Yes, I am well on my way to achieving financial independence. Notice, however, that financial independence is not mentioned until my fifth priority.

That's not to say that money isn't important to me. I want to make money because of the personal freedom and security it provides. But financial wealth is not my end goal.

For those who list financial wealth as their number one goals, the journey is often much harder. These people might say, "I want to make ten million dollars and retire by age fifty; I don't care how I make the money, I just want to make it." They then spend twenty to thirty years toiling and slaving to make that money. Very often, they burn out, or sometimes even work themselves to death, before they can enjoy the fruits of their labor. When they do reach that coveted sum and are able to retire, many times they look around and say to themselves, "Okay, I've got all this money, but I have no idea how to use it to enjoy life as I've always wanted to."

I personally think it's better to work for a more modest but steady income doing work that I enjoy and believe in than to spend years working for a targeted sum of $X million that I may never reach. I want to enjoy the quality of my journey through life. I've done this by achieving my first reason, my desire to build a good communications company. The money has come only as a result of achieving this goal.

I can't tell you how good it feels to be on the road to achieving most of my business and personal goals. I know that much of what I've accomplished has come with the help and counsel of numerous other people. I also realize that it could all end tomorrow. I certainly hope not, but it could. But that's all the more reason for me to keep working towards my goals. Since my business provides me with the quality of life I enjoy, I will enjoy my life while it lasts.

~

Having owned my own business for over twenty-five years, I now wouldn't trade it for anything.

~

I'd find it difficult, if not impossible, to go back to the 9 a.m. to 5 p.m. routine. It's not that I can't work for anyone else. When you're self-employed, you often work for many people at once. Like a politician, you sometimes have more "bosses" than you did when you worked for a regular company. But having owned my own business, I would now have a very hard time going back to work in the daily structure of corporate business, a structure I think is wasteful and outdated.

What are your five reasons for self-employment?

When hard times come, it's important to have good reasons for putting yourself through the grind of sustaining your own business. It's not enough just to say, "I have my own reasons for being self-employed." You have to *feel* those reasons and *believe* in them in order to reaffirm your efforts. If you can't think of at least five good reasons why you want to be self-employed, it will be better to stick with your day job.

Again, the most essential question to ask yourself is why you want to start your own business in the first place? Is it money? Is it independence? Or do you have an incredible concept that you want to launch and turn into a business?

Write them down now:

1. _____
   _____
   _____

2. _____
   _____
   _____

3. _____

   _____

   _____

4. _____

   _____

   _____

5. _____

   _____

   _____

Preflight Checklist

THE 4 TRUTHS
ABOUT EXPERIENCE

Truth #1: Experience is key

If you don't have a traditional "strong business background," you might think starting your own business is beyond your grasp. But you'd be wrong! Again, I'm living proof that you don't need an MBA to be a successful businessman. I graduated from Washington State University with a degree in political science. While at WSU, I also took a number of communications and political science courses, but I didn't take any courses on running a business.

But good judgment and organization skills take time to acquire. I strongly believe that *experience* is a major factor for starting a successful business. Understand, I'm not talking about business experience, although it certainly doesn't hurt if you have some. I'm talking about *life experience*. The more you know about the way things work—on the job, at home, and in the world in general—the better equipped you'll be to start your own business. Unfortunately, experience is an attribute you can only acquire with age.

Truth #2: Experience is acquired

The Civil War movie *Glory* makes a great point about experience. The movie tells the story of the 54th Massachusetts Infantry, the first all-African-American regiment to serve in the United States Army. In one scene, the regiment recruits have just been issued their musket rifles and are taking target practice. One soldier, Private Jupiter Sharts (played by Jihmi Kennedy), is able to hit the bulls-eye consistently. His fellow soldiers (who include Denzel Washington, Morgan Freeman, and Andre Braugher) are impressed with his marksmanship. Private Sharts explains proudly that he learned how to shoot while hunting squirrels.

The regiment commander, Colonel Robert Gould Shaw (Matthew Broderick), who earlier in the film was wounded in the hellish battle of Antietam, hears this. He instructs Private Sharts to reload his rifle and fire it as quickly as he can. "A good soldier can load and fire his rifle three times in one minute," Shaw tells the assembled soldiers. Private Sharts quickly reloads his rifle, pouring gunpowder from his powder horn onto the flintlock and using a ramrod to push the bullet down the long barrel. As he does this, Colonel Shaw suddenly pulls out a pistol and begins firing gunshots in the air just behind Sharts's ear, simulating the sounds that the soldiers will hear in battle. Sharts is frightened and nervously drops his rifle.

In this scene, Colonel Shaw teaches his troops that they will only become effective soldiers when they've experienced the chaos and ear-splitting noise of battle first-hand. It is one thing to stand on a firing range and score a bull's-eye on a target fifty yards away and under ideal conditions. It is something else to load your rifle, aim at a moving target, shoot, and then reload your rifle in the middle of a real battle.

The point is experience is something that can only be acquired, not learned.

As with soldiers in battle, a certain amount of experience is necessary to be an effective business owner (although hopefully, as a business owner, you'll never have to load and fire a musket). You can put together a dynamic business plan with a timetable for creating your products and/or building your clientele and rosy projections for annual increased profits over the next five years. But the real challenge is to make it work. I am sad to report that in about 80 percent of the cases it doesn't work.

There are dozens of factors—everything from local and national economic growth to marketability of your product or service, from the corporate calendars of your clients to your annual decrease or increase of expenses—that will affect your business. The more you know about your own business, and about the world in general, the better prepared you will be to start your own business and sustain it for the long run. The best time to start your own business is when you have some experience under your belt.

Truth #3: Timing is everything

If I were to pick an ideal age for a person to start his or her own business, I would say early- to mid-30s.

No one should try to start a business right out of college (or worse right out of high school). A college education will give you the facts you need, but not the experience. Understand, I'm not saying you *shouldn't* go to college. Having any college degree will serve you well in starting your own business. And higher education teaches you necessary skills like discipline, organization, and option thinking (a crucial skill when you have your own business).

~

But higher education is usually more about theory than actual job experience.

~

For example, if you've just earned a BA in Marketing, chances are you know the fundamentals of marketing. But if someone were to ask you to put together a marketing campaign for a new brand of toothpaste, or a line of color copiers, or an investment firm, you probably wouldn't be able to do it correctly. You might be able to manage the individual elements—i.e., market research, brand design, advertising, and promotion planning—but you lack the experience needed to create an effective marketing campaign from scratch. Only by getting a marketing-related job, and by learning on the job how to organize a marketing campaign, will you acquire the skills you need to start your own marketing consulting business.

Before I go on, I want to interject a disclaimer. If you've grown up in a family of entrepreneurs, you have a tremendous advantage over the rest of us. You've probably watched very closely the rewards and difficulties of running a small business. In this case, starting your own business in your twenties isn't a negative. You're already a lap ahead of the rest of the pack.

In your twenties, you are still figuring out what you want to do in life and also what you *don't* want to do in life. Give yourself time to experiment, to see what type of career or which area of your chosen profession is right for you. Then, once you've decided, learn how to do your job right before you try to make a business out of it.

When you reach your thirties, you have typically acquired the "street smarts" it takes to start a business and make it grow. Whatever profession you've chosen, you now have enough experience to call yourself an "expert" in your field. If you're an advertising agent, you've probably worked for several agencies creating ad campaigns. If you want to start a digital consulting service, you've probably already worked for several digital companies and are familiar with the current technologies. If you want to sell wooden boats, cat toys, alpaca sweaters, etc., you may already be creating and/or selling your product in your spare time and would like to go full-time with your business.

Also, in your thirties, you know how to "have a job." You know how to plan your work, organize each task, and get it done to meet your deadlines or quotas. You know how to have an effective meeting with your supervisors, how to talk with them and listen to them, and how to satisfy them with your job performance. When they aren't satisfied, you probably know how to analyze your work and correct the problem to their satisfaction. (As a self-employed business owner, these kinds of skills will serve you well in dealing with your clients or customers.)

You may have even lost a job or two, at some point. Perhaps you've been fired or laid off or had an employment contract end too soon due to a budget cut or an employer's bad whim. Believe it or not, this is good! If you were able to get back on your feet and find a new job, you have experience in "coming back." That is, you know how to rebuild your life and your career after suffering a setback. (And if you've ever been fired from a job for a mistake you made, at least you know what that mistake is, and can avoid making it again in the future.)

In your thirties, you also have enough life experience to know how the world works. You know how to manage your personal schedule. You enjoy being around people and can talk to them easily. You have probably exercised judgment in making some major lifestyle decisions, such as what type of house or car to buy or whether or not to go back to school for an advanced degree. If you are married and have kids, you're accustomed to managing daily responsibilities, even under chaos situations.

Life experiences help you keep your perspective in bad times and in good times. With your life experience, you've probably developed a perspective on the world—that is, a way of seeing how the world works and how your life works. You can look into the future and see the possible outcomes and potential consequences of your courses of action. A good perspective of your life will serve you well as a self-employed business owner. It will enable you to see your business for what it is and how well or how badly it is doing.

As a self-employed business owner, I've lived on very little income and I've lived with plenty of income. I know what it's like to make serious choices about whether to stay in business or close the doors. I have felt the pain and made it through the rough spots. All this experience has given me some perspective on how to start a business and keep it going through hard times. Perspective is an extremely valuable attribute, and perspective comes with experience.

~

Running your business day-to-day is raw. You are never more exposed.

~

Success and failure are both very evident and decisive. Either you eventually make it or you don't. It can be a very long or short struggle. But if you don't adhere to certain basic principals, your business will eventually die. Guaranteed!

Truth #4: Learn from mistakes

We all have regrets. As we get older, we can look back with some perspective and see how we might have done things differently. We can only hope that when we failed, we learned from that failure and took corrective action the next time we were confronted with similar circumstances.

I have a personal maxim that you cannot call a mistake a "mistake" unless you allow yourself to make it more than once.

~

**The first time you make any kind
of mistake, it is really a "misstep."
You have no previous experience
to use as a point of reference.**

~

As a business owner, you must make decisions all the time, and some of your decisions will turn out to be wrong. Your wrong decisions are the "missteps," the experiences that you learn from. Later on, when a similar situation arises in your business, hopefully you'll know better than to make the same misstep a second time. But if you *don't* learn from your previous misstep, if you allow yourself to make the same misstep the second time around, *then* it's a mistake!

What do I mean by this? Well, here's an example from my own experience. As I've already mentioned, when I was publishing my newspaper, one of my advertisers, a retirement center, went out of business without paying me and stuck me with a printing bill for $10,000. Before this retirement center went bankrupt, I started noticing "trouble signs"—late payments, unreturned phone calls, etc. But I continued to extend them credit by running their ads in my newspaper. That was my "misstep." I didn't see that my client was having financial trouble until it was too late.

About ten years later, I had a similar experience. I was working with a travel agency, developing radio ad campaigns and buying airtime for their commercials. As part of my service to my clients, I normally purchase airtime "on credit" from the radio stations that I work with. The radio stations reserve the airtime and run the commercials. The client then pays me after the commercials have run, and I pay the radio stations. If ever a client doesn't pay me, then I have to pay the radio stations for the airtime out of my own pocket. If I don't, my credit is pulled, and I wouldn't be able to establish credit on any radio station in the entire country. That would be a severe or fatal blow to my company.

I started noticing some of the same trouble signs with the travel agency that I had noticed with my previous client who went bankrupt. The travel agency was suddenly very late in making payments to me. Their payments started arriving every two to three months, instead of once a month as usual. I sensed the travel agency was having financial troubles. So after being paid in full for my most recent ad campaign, I informed the owner of the travel agency that I would have to receive the money for future ad campaigns up front if I was to continue our relationship. The owner said he couldn't do this. I wished him well but said I could no longer work with his company. A few months later, I received a notice in the mail that the travel agency had declared bankruptcy.

By reading the trouble signs correctly, I avoided making

the same misstep with the travel agency that I'd made with the retirement center. If I'd kept on doing business with the travel agency, even after my experience with the previous client, *that* would have been a mistake! If the travel agency had gone out of business without paying me, I would've once again been forced to pay my vendors, in this case the radio stations, out of my own pocket. But because of my previous experience with the other client, I was able to avoid making this mistake.

Preflight Checklist

THE 3 POINTS ON
ETHICS AND INTEGRITY

··

My parents taught me ethics and integrity, just as their parents taught *them* the importance of honesty. I consider myself lucky to have grown up in a family environment where doing the right thing was considered to be the *only* option. If you have to think long and hard about the difference between right and wrong, then starting a business may not be the best thing for you.

~

Ethics is defined as: The rules and standards governing the conduct of members of a profession. Integrity is defined as: Strict personal honesty and independence.

~

The only part of life you have absolute control over is your word. If you work for a large organization, you can sometimes hide from ethics. Under the company umbrella, you are not considered to be entirely "at fault" for the company's unethical decisions. You may have been one of several hundred unethical decision-makers. Even if you knew the decisions you were making were wrong, you may have been in a position where you were forced to make those decisions or lose your job.

The movie, *Margin Call*, provides a great example of this. It's about a New York investment banking firm, based on Merrill Lynch and Lehman Brothers. In 2008, the bankers at this company (played by Kevin Spacey, Demi Moore, Paul Bettany, Zachary Quinto, and Stanley Tucci) discover that the amount of debt owned by the company is more than the company itself is worth, thanks to their recent drive to sell subprime mortgages. The bankers realize their company is about to collapse, which will trigger a financial meltdown of the US economy. Looking at the mess they've created, the bankers realize that they are *all* responsible for it. Everyone at the company knew these subprime mortgages were a bad deal, but they kept selling them as a way of making quick profits.

But as a self-employed business owner, you are 100 percent accountable for your own actions! When things go wrong due to an ethical lapse, the only finger you can point is at yourself! If you are ethically challenged, I can absolutely guarantee it will catch up with you at some point.

There will come a point in your life where you must decide if you will be up-front and honest with people, or if you will do anything to make a buck. Having a creed of ethics and integrity is a conscious mindset. Your goal should be to place ethics and integrity into your *unconscious* mindset as well, so this creed becomes automatic to you.

Don't go into business for yourself unless you have a strong sense of ethics and integrity. I've made my share of business mistakes, but I've always made a point of adhering to ethics and integrity. If a client overpays me by even just a dollar, my accountant is under strict instructions to return the money. If I give you my word, nothing will stop me from trying to fulfill that commitment. If I fail, I will apologize and take full responsibility for my shortcomings.

Point #1: Action says it all

If a coach breaks a contract with a college athletic department and leaps to another institution for a huge amount of money, many people seem to be indifferent about it. I hear people say, "Anyone would do what he did." This is so not true! I know of plenty of coaches who believe teaching is their primary mission. They realize if they abandon their contracts, they will abandon their commitments to the athletes, to the students they've recruited. They know if they walk away from their word, they're making a hugely negative lifestyle statement to the young people they coach.

I used to hear that executives would play golf with prospective executive recruits before they even considered hiring them. When I first heard about this, I assumed that the boss was trying to show the recruit how great his life could be if he worked hard. I found out otherwise when I started playing golf in my late twenties. Golf is a game of honor. You keep your own score, and therefore it's easy to shade a few strokes. Anyone who plays the game will tell you how frustrating it can be. A really good shot can be quickly wiped out by a bad shot.

An executive or business owner can learn a lot about potential recruits, business partners, and possible future associates during a four-hour-plus round of golf. You can find out if they are honest. Do they keep their score accurately? You can learn about their temperaments. Can they control their tempers, or do they pitch their nine-irons into the lake after making a bad shot? You can also learn about how they deal with setbacks. After making bad shots, can they concentrate on making the next ones? Between holes, you find out how they think about things outside the workplace and what's important to them. In golf, you can learn a lot about people outside the business environment.

I'm not suggesting that you should necessarily take all your potential business associates out for a round of golf, but you should observe how your associates and potential clients think and act while doing business with you. Actions speak louder than words. Observing how someone makes an ethical choice or reacts in a situation will tell you if that person is someone you should do business with or associate with. What a person does will often give you more insight into his or her true character than what he or she says.

Point #2: Confidence versus arrogance

~

If you own a business, self-confidence is not an option; it's an absolute must!

~

You must be confident about yourself as a person and demonstrate that confidence to others. You can't expect other people to follow your lead if you yourself don't believe strongly in your own skills and in your product or service.

But there's a fine line between confidence and arrogance. Arrogance is the quality of being too confident, of believing no client can do without your product or service and you're the only person in the world who can provide them with it. Like confidence, people pick up on arrogance very quickly. If a client senses you are patronizing them, or if you treat them as if they aren't intelligent enough to understand the benefits of your product or service, it's very easy for them to turn you down. Usually, they give you a standard excuse (e.g., "We just don't have the budget for this."), but they never tell you the real reason why they're refusing you.

Arrogance is also assuming your business is going to succeed and not having a backup plan in case something goes wrong. Again, if you think you have an absolute, can't-miss, guaranteed business, it might be a good idea to stop and think about what could conceivably go wrong with it. Pay special attention if you find yourself examining a potential problem and saying, "That could never happen."

Disasters and setbacks often come from the places we least expect. Chances are, what you think could never happen, can and will happen.

Remember the lesson of the *Titanic* which I referred to earlier in the book. There weren't enough lifeboats for all the passengers on the ship, because the ship itself was thought to be "unsinkable." When the ship actually did sink after hitting an iceberg, the lack of lifeboats resulted in a huge, catastrophic loss of life.

Don't let the risks of business overwhelm you, but don't underestimate them either. You can't eliminate risk; you can only minimize your exposure to it.

Point #3: Is the glass half empty?

At times, business people seem to wear blinders. They see the glass as half-empty when it's really half-full—or even three-quarters full! I once had a budget of about $135,000 to spend on a radio campaign in a major metropolitan region. One radio group in this particular market received over $100,000 of the buy. The rest of the radio groups in this market received a combined total of $33,000. Obviously, the radio group that received $100,000 was the largest radio group and had the largest number of listeners that I was trying to reach on behalf of my client.

After the $100,000 radio group learned of my intended buy, I received a call from their sales manager. I thought he would be ecstatic with my decision.

Instead, the first words out of his mouth were literally: "This is unacceptable!"

For a moment, I thought he was kidding. When I realized he was not joking, I told him I was expecting an important call and would have to get back to him tomorrow. I said this because I had to cool down before speaking to him. I was so angry that I was afraid I might say something I would later regret. (I have a "24-hour rule." If I am going to say anything negative, I will wait at least twenty-four hours.)

When I finally got back to the sales manager, he said that he felt that his radio group deserved a larger percentage of the buy in this particular market.

He went on to say that the $100,000 buy would make them short of their income projections. I took notes, politely said goodbye, and hung up.

Then I called a salesperson I knew at the station and asked her to tell the sales director that if they didn't reserve the time for the radio purchase by noon that day, the whole deal was off.

They reserved the time.

~

As I've said before, one of my major reasons for starting my own business was to achieve freedom of association, the freedom to choose the people I will and will not work with.

~

There are certain people I just won't do business with anymore. This includes people who don't get back to you after you've contacted them a couple of times. It also includes people who haggle over the cost of every small detail of your work for them, people who keep you waiting for months on end while they make up their minds whether or not they're going to do the project they've hired you for, people who cancel meetings with you at the last minute, and people who don't send you all the material you need to do the job right. It also includes people who take several months to pay you once you've completed the job. You have to keep calling them back and maybe send two or three invoices before they send you the check they had promised to send you three weeks ago.

On the other hand, it's a real joy to work with people who pay their bills on time, so you don't wake up at 3 a.m. wondering if you will get paid in time to pay your own bills. It's a pleasure to work with people who are accountable, who meet their deadlines, who always keep their word, and who go out of their way to let you know that they appreciate your business. Life is so much easier when you work with people like this. Your distress level goes down, and the quality of your journey is greatly enhanced. It's much more pleasant to do business with someone if you really like him or her. The great news is, the vast majority of business people fit into this category.

Preflight Checklist

THE 4 PITFALLS
OF PARTNERSHIPS

....

Real entrepreneurs don't need partners. Partnerships destroy businesses and are counterproductive to sustaining your business. It's human nature to want a friend or confidant to go down the unknown path with you, but resist this temptation at all costs.

If you feel you must have a partner to succeed, you probably don't have the necessary confidence or independence it takes to be successful in business anyway.

Many people feel obligated to take on a partner because they feel the partner will bring camaraderie or some knowledge or skill to the business that they don't have. But often, this "essential knowledge or skill" can be found elsewhere. For instance, you might feel it's necessary to bring in a partner with strong accounting skills, because you yourself have no background in accounting. But it would be easier and less expensive in the long run to find a free agent accountant or bookkeeper instead.

~

The problem with partnerships is that you are essentially giving away half your business before you start.

~

Generally, under a partnership agreement, your partner receives half of all income for your business. If you earn $2,000 on a project, your partner receives $1,000 of that, whether the partner did any work on the project or not. Of course, the reverse may be true. You could be receiving half the money your partner earned on an assignment for which you did nothing. But it would be much better to keep the $2,000 (minus expenses) you've earned, instead of instantly giving half of it away.

If you and your partner are working together on assignments, you are invariably providing your clients with two workers for the price of one. For example, say you own a marketing consulting firm, and a local software company pays you $5,000 to develop a marketing plan. You and your partner do equal work on the project and split the $5,000. However, as a marketing specialist, you could have just as easily created a marketing plan all by yourself and earned the same $5,000 as a sole business owner. If you're an expert at what you do—if you have the competence to deliver a good product or service and enough experience to be able to start your own business— you don't need to share your job duties or your profits with a partner.

With partnerships, the double expenses cut severely into your business. Each partner receives only a fraction of the profit that either of them would receive as a sole proprietor. This combination of high expenses and low profits makes it extremely difficult for a business to survive in the long term.

Pitfall #1: Decision making

Aside from the financial obligations, a partnership can bring other problems. First, a partner adds another layer to the decision-making process. You will always need your partner's approval before taking on any new clients, investing in new technologies, subscribing to new services, etc. Inevitably, there will be clashes between partners over which clients to deal with, who to hire and fire, how to provide the best product or service to your clients, etc. It's much better for the business if one person is in charge and has the power to make the decisions.

As I've said before, businesses change over time. The business you start today will be vastly different from the business you will have five years from now. It will change and grow and move in many different directions. Even if you and your partner have the same vision and goals for your business today, your separate visions and goals will inevitably change as the years go by. Before long, the odds are that you'll want to move your business in one direction, while your partner will want to move the business in another direction. I've seen most partnerships work for only short periods of time. Invariably, they break apart when the partners can't agree on the best way to further develop and continue their business together.

If the business survives the breakup, one of the partners usually inherits the business. The partner who takes over the company is now in the same position they would have been in if they'd started the business without a partner in the first place. The only difference is, now they may have to buy the other partner out. The expense of buying out one-half of a partnership increases your overhead and only makes it more difficult to make money in the future.

Pitfall #2: Working family

Even if a partnership defies the odds and lasts longer than usual, something will inevitably happen to break up the business. If a partner dies (as sometimes happens), very often his or her half of the partnership will be acquired by his or her spouse or children. In such a case, your partner's wife, husband, or children may actually end up being your business partner(s). There are numerous horror stories of a partner's family members inheriting half of the business and ruining it because they are only interested in its assets and have no interest in running the business itself.

Having a partner brings too many negative elements to your business, elements that can severely inhibit your success. It's best to avoid these elements and go it alone.

~

As a sole business owner, you alone will be responsible for your success or failure.

~

Again, this may seem scary at times, but it's actually an advantage. With a partnership, you must work twice as hard to make your business successful and overcome twice the disadvantages. Your business will always be dependent on your partner's success as well as your own.

As a sole business owner, you at least have the freedom to try, to fail, and to try again without encountering the disadvantages of having a partner.

Avoid including friends and family in the day-to-day operations of your business. Your parents, brothers, and sisters can be your best allies but also your worst critics. While they may outwardly support your efforts, they often think you're slightly crazy to be starting your own business and wonder when you will go back to a "real job." When they give you advice, they might think they're doing what is best for you, but their comments can be very harmful.

"Well, you know, you never were very good at this or that." "I don't really think you can make a living doing what you're doing." "You never could balance a checkbook." Families and friends are for Thanksgiving and Christmas.

~

Never go into business with a family member or a friend.

~

Just because you have a personal or family relationship with someone, it doesn't mean they will make a good business partner, nor does it mean they will necessarily have sound business advice for you. I'm very grateful to my own family because they've always been hands-off in the day-to-day operations of my business. If you want advice about your business, talk to a small-business consultant or to someone who runs a small business with a product or service similar to yours.

Pitfall #3: Advisors

Another business killer is appointing a board of directors or advisors with formal or informal oversight responsibilities of your business operations. I've read business books about starting your own business that suggest you should appoint a board of directors to meet monthly or quarterly to provide you with counsel and advice for your business. I couldn't disagree more.

As a self-employed business owner, you probably don't need to worry about appointing a board of directors, even if your business is successful enough that turning it into a corporation seems viable. Boards are for large corporations and non-profits that can afford the slow decision-making process. Boards often spend their time telling you what you *shouldn't* do, rather than what you should do. They prevent you from making decisions, and also from making mistakes. As I've said before, it's better to try new things and learn from your mistakes than it is to spend all your time trying to avoid mistakes and thus accomplishing nothing.

~

When you own your own business, *you* are the decision-maker.

~

This is a huge responsibility, but it's also a competitive advantage. You can get things done faster and with less trouble than you would in a large corporation. It may be difficult to suddenly find yourself in the role of sole decision-maker, especially if you've just left a corporate or government job where a large staff or board of directors made all the important decisions. But the sooner you get into the habit of being a decision-maker on your own, the better off you will be.

While you shouldn't bother with a board of directors, it may help you to occasionally think of yourself as a "Chairperson of the Board" and to ask yourself the kinds of questions a board of directors would ask (e.g., Where do we want our business to be in six months? What goals would we like to accomplish in the next year that weren't accomplished last year?).

It may sound strange, but I sometimes hold "board meetings," featuring only myself, to answer questions like these and to plan strategies for the growth of my business. I sit alone in my office and ask myself questions as if I were addressing an invisible board of directors. This way, I'm able to clarify my thoughts about various problems and examine my options for solving them. (I usually keep the office door closed during these "board meetings" so the people in neighboring offices won't look in and think they should call the men in the white coats.)

Pitfall #4: Franchises

Franchises are a different kind of partnership, but one that seems to have a higher success rate than partnerships between friends and business associates. With franchises, you are partnering with a local or national company instead of another person. Most are food franchises, followed by weight-loss programs, home services, cleaning, glass repair, and printing companies. Two-thirds of reporting franchises have been in business for twelve years or more. Retail food franchises seem to have the longest duration. Economic downturns result in an increase in franchises.[9]

The advantage of a franchise is that it provides an established formula and in many cases is built on a strong brand name. Franchises are pre-packaged like modular homes, and customers go to franchises because they like the familiarity. If you walk into a Subway restaurant in Grand Rapids, Michigan, you'll get the same food as you would in a Subway in Grand Forks, North Dakota, or in the Subway in Grand Central Station in New York. And the interiors of these restaurants look pretty much the same, no matter where you go. Franchise owners typically have to do very little marketing to promote their businesses. Since I believe that many businesses fail because of a limited knowledge of marketing, franchises can be valuable for this reason alone.

---

[9] Alf Nucifora, "The Franchising Industry Continues to Heighten," *Alf Nucifora* (web log), http://www.nucifora.com/art_170.html.

~

But buying into a franchise also means you are beholden to the parent company. Your success is limited by the demand for your particular franchise in your area and by your employees' ability to do their jobs well.

~

I recommend, prior to partnering with any franchise, that you should try starting a business on your own. If you follow the principles outlined in this book—keeping low overhead, trusting your instincts, testing your concepts, etc.—you may be able to create a successful independent business. Then, if you wish, you can partner with a franchise in the future. Not only will you have experience in the business, you'll also be in a position to negotiate what you need from the franchise and to eliminate what you don't need.

Before making any franchise agreement, talk to franchise owners in your area who have franchises similar to the one you are thinking of buying. Find out how well their particular franchises have done in your area and how successful their relationships have been with the parent companies. Make sure you ask a good business attorney to look over the franchise agreement before you sign it.

~

Keep in close communication with the parent company from which you buy the franchise.

~

But be cautious! Don't automatically assume that everything they tell you about how to set up and run your franchise is necessarily true or correct. Obviously, their formula for success has been duplicated many times. But when your gut instinct tells you the parent company is wrong, trust your gut instinct!

I have a friend named Sally who bought into a printing franchise about ten years ago. She decided to open a print shop when she noticed a shortage of qualified printers in her immediate area. She heard that a national print chain was expanding to the West Coast. The printing chain required a hefty down payment with high monthly consulting fees, so Sally took out a second mortgage on her home and partnered with them.

The printing chain recommended a location about ten miles south of the community where Sally had envisioned the need for a print shop. Sally didn't understand the choice of the location but decided to trust the chain's recommendation. After all, they were the experts. She was sure the national chain had good reasons for selecting this location (e.g., foot traffic, easy access for surrounding businesses, etc.).

But after the doors opened at her new print shop, Sally quickly learned that there were other highly competitive print shops in the immediate area. She had signed a long-term lease agreement with a high monthly rent, but the customer base just wasn't there. When she needed assistance, the national printing chain offered very little help. They didn't have a strong market presence in the first place, and it was expensive for them to send a representative out to the West Coast to help her.

In retrospect, Sally should have trusted her instincts despite the national chain's recommendation. She should have looked for inexpensive retail space in the area where she first saw the need for a print shop. Instead of a long-term lease, she could have signed a six-month lease with an option to renew for three to five years. She could have then leased used printing equipment and supplied her future clients with very basic printing needs. By keeping her overhead low and testing her concept slowly, she could have stayed in business long enough to find out if the print shop could work in the location that she had chosen.

Because Sally knew the neighborhood (and because she has a great personality and is very efficient), she could have gone door-to-door and personally met with her future clients. After several months, Sally would have known if the print shop location would be successful. She could have then extended her lease and upgraded the printing equipment over time.

If, after several months, Sally discovered she had made a mistake in location, or if the customer base wasn't there to sustain a printing business, she could have shut down the operation and returned the leased printing equipment with minimal financial loss. She would now know a lot more about the printing business and could have made another go of it in another location. With a short lease, she could have moved quickly.

Unfortunately, after losing a ton of money with her print shop, Sally was forced to close her doors. However, I'm happy to report she has since landed on her feet and is now stronger than ever. It turned out many of her clients at the print shop had a need for a graphic artist. Since Sally has a talent in this area, she started doing graphics work on the side. When the print shop closed, she had a client base to launch a graphics design firm. In recent years, she has expanded her business to provide clients with reproductions of old graphic art from 18th-century books.

The bad experience of my friend Sally might not be typical of franchises. Many franchise owners would probably tell you they are very satisfied with their businesses. While franchises may provide a different business model than self-employment, the franchise owner can still benefit from applying the principles outlined in this book. Keeping overhead low, testing your concepts, and trusting your business instincts will help your business to prosper in the long run, and can help you to escape disasters, no matter what type of business you have.

THE 7 TIPS ON FINANCES

....

Tip #1: Keep your overhead low

As a self-employed business owner, keeping your expenses at an absolute minimum is essential for the survival of your business. As we've already seen, many businesses fail because their overhead is just too high. The dot-coms in particular were notorious for losing hundreds of millions of dollars because they didn't have the slightest concern or discipline for controlling their money. Their losses were equated to a "burn rate." If you are self-employed, a burn rate is the equivalent of watching your business go up in smoke.

Be absolutely ruthless in hanging on to every dollar you own. Again, before you make any huge purchases, ask yourself how much your business really needs what you are buying and whether or not you can get along without it. Look around for bargains. Check second-hand stores and outlets for low-priced office furniture, look around at surplus houses for used computers and electronic equipment, and try to buy office supplies wholesale. Let the big boys sit in the glass towers, drive expensive cars, and strategize about how and when to launch an IPO. By limiting your expenditures to necessities and avoiding luxuries as you build your business, you can avoid the trouble spots that often plague start-ups.

~

Keeping your overhead low doesn't mean being cheap.

~

It just means knowing how to spend your money wisely and where to invest. For example, it's critical that you have a good appearance when you meet with potential clients or customers. You don't have to spend $2,500 on a business suit, but you shouldn't spend $99 either. Instead, you could spend $650 to $850 on two or three high-quality suits, rather than five cheap suits.

Tip #2: Create a bare-bones budget

How much money do you really need to start your business? It depends on what type of business you start. My best advice is to make a list of the bare minimum that you need to get your business going, and stick to that list. Don't make any huge investments to build your business until you know if it's going to work or not.

I had about $20,000 when I started my business over twenty-five years ago. One reason I started out as a publisher was that publishing didn't require a huge cash outlay up front. I didn't need to sign a long-term lease agreement for equipment or office space. The success of my newspaper rested largely on my imagination for strong editorial content and on my ability to sell advertising. If I'd found I wasn't able to cut it in either department, I could have easily shut the business down with minimal loss.

Before you start your business, it's best to make sure that your personal expenses will be taken care of, as well as your business expenses. If you decide to quit your job, it's a good idea to have enough money saved to cover about six months' worth of expenses before taking the plunge into full-time entrepreneurship.

Even if your spouse works and has agreed to support the family while you are building your business, it's best to have money in reserve to cover your expenses, in case something goes wrong (e.g., your spouse loses his or her job or is suddenly no longer able to work).

Tip #3: Forget banks

If you think banks will help you to finance your business, think again. With banks, the general rule is: If you need the money, it's not available. If you don't need the money, bank lenders will break down your door trying to lend it to you.

~

Banks don't trust entrepreneurs because they don't have a "traditional job," meaning an eight-to-five office job with a regular pre-determined salary.

~

It doesn't matter if you've been in business for fifteen years, are making excellent profits, and have a stellar credit history. If you try to borrow money, bank lenders look at you as if you have some kind of infectious disease.

There was a time when I earned three times as much income as my wife. (Today, I'm happy to say, our annual incomes are more or less equal.) Yet when we financed the original mortgage for our house, our banks still considered her to be the main breadwinner of the household, because she worked for a large company and had a "real job."

In my opinion, a person who has run a business successfully for an extended period of time is less of a risk than someone who has a so-called "steady job." An entrepreneur can be very resourceful in making payments to his or her billers and creditors when the money gets tight.

Someone who loses a steady or secure job, on the other hand, is like a deer in the headlights. This person freezes and thinks the whole world has suddenly come to an end!

But banks don't see it that way. In their minds, if you're a small business owner, the failure of your business is just around the corner. (After all, you could walk out the bank door and have an anvil drop on your head.)

I don't want to be overly negative about banks. With an 80 percent failure rate of small businesses, it is understandable that they are very, very cautious. I would be too.

If you wish to finance your own business, your best options are:

❏ Money from your personal savings (best option)

❏ A loan from a relative.

❏ A second mortgage. Banks will always give you a second mortgage on property you own, although they may charge you a slightly higher interest rate.

Tip #4: Try crowdfunding

Since I wrote the first edition of this book, a new Internet phenomenon known as "crowdfunding" has taken root. Crowdfunding gives small businesses and organizations access to funding opportunities by connecting entrepreneurs with investors and venture capitalists. It can be used for financing startup businesses, inventor's innovations, and new technologies, as well as non-profit or community-based projects (e.g., renovation of a local park), arts projects (e.g., movies or music albums), and charities (e.g., funding for cancer treatments).

With crowdfunding, you create a campaign on a crowdfunding site. The campaign includes a fundraising goal (e.g., $10,000) and a time period (e.g., sixty days) in which you will accept donations. You also create a profile of the campaign, which may include a description of a product or service you'd like to develop or a project you'd like to do (e.g., a book or a film), a business plan, and highlights of your skills and experience in this area. Finally, you create a tiered set of rewards for your "angel investors" based on the amounts they donate to your campaign.

The idea behind crowdfunding is, instead of looking for one investor to give you a huge amount of money, you look for dozens, or even hundreds, of investors to give you small amounts of money, which will add up to your fundraising goal. Hence the term "crowdfunding," since you are being funded by a crowd.

There are literally over 400 crowdfunding sites on the Web. The most popular sites are Kickstarter, Indiegogo, LaunchGood, RocketHub, and GoFundMe. Some crowdsourcing sites provide funding specifically for small businesses and entrepreneurship, including AngelList, Crowdfunder, Invest Next Door, Wefunder, and MoolaHoop (for women entrepreneurs). And some sites focus specifically on crowdfunding for tech startups, including MicroVentures, RockthePost, SeedInvest, StartupValley, and AppBackr (for computer app developers).

I've done a bit of research on crowdfunding. It can be a good source of financing for small business ventures—if you know how to do it right. But there are several things you need to understand about crowdfunding. (I give you a few basic pointers below, but I suggest you do your own research on how to do crowdfunding before launching a campaign.)

First, crowdfunding is not a guarantee of instant funding. Even if you have a great business idea or a new product to market, you can't just put out a campaign on a crowdfunding site and expect "angel investors" to flock right to you, giving you instant seed money. Many crowdfunding campaigns are unsuccessful. They raise only a minimal amount of money, usually nowhere near the amount that the entrepreneur or organization needs to make the project happen.

According to Kickstarter, only about one-third of the 70,000+ campaigns posted annually on its site get funded. The general consensus is, the less money you ask for, the easier it is to reach your goal. Kickstarter says that about 73 percent of the *successful* campaigns on its site received $10,000 or less, while only 2 percent of the successful campaigns received $100,000 or more. So you need to be realistic about your crowdfunding expectations.

Second, crowdfunding campaigns work best for companies

that already have a substantial following. A month or two before you launch your campaign, you should start to get the word out to friends, family, and customers or clients. Let them know what the crowdfunding campaign is about, what your funding goal is, and the kickoff date. Most successful crowdfunding campaigns are able to get about 30 percent of their fundraising goal pre-committed before the campaign starts.

Before (and during) the campaign, you should be constantly promoting it. Use social media, email marketing, word-of-mouth, etc. Do guest blogging and contact media sources. But get the word out *before* you launch the campaign, so you can build interest in it. When the campaign launches, send out multiple announcements, especially to those who have already committed to making donations, reminding them that the campaign is live and that they should continue to donate more if they can to help you reach your goal. And keep promoting for the entire length of the campaign, until it's over.

Also, before the campaign, you need to refine your profile on the crowdfunding site as much as possible. Make yourself and your business idea stand out from the thousands of other entrepreneurs, inventors, and would-be artists asking for funding on these sites. If you have a solid and unique business idea, explain how you plan to execute the idea once you receive funding. If you have an innovative new product or technology, explain how it works or how it will make an existing product work better (e.g., if it's a new business app for mobile phones). If you can add photos or a video to your profile to illustrate your concepts or highlight past examples of your work, all the better.

Finally, think long and hard about what types of rewards you will offer in your tiered rewards system for the crowdfunding campaign. You need to offer rewards that will be of value to customers and will make them want to donate substantial amounts to your campaign. (Two notes on this: 1) Many successful crowdfunding campaigns have involved the sale of a gadget, such as a video game, in which the investors were able to use the funding campaign to pre-order the product that would be created as a result of it. In other words, in return for helping to finance the creation of the video game, they received a copy of the game as a reward. 2) Some crowdfunding sites for entrepreneurs and startups have an equity-based rewards system with which investors receive a stake in your startup company and receive dividends when the company becomes successful. Other crowdfunding sites have a debt-based rewards system with which you agree to repay investors who make loans to you for your business ventures.)

Since this phenomenon started, I've personally had a few experiences with crowdfunding campaigns. Not long ago, my wife and I went out for dinner at The Plum Bistro, one of our favorite vegetarian restaurants, located in Seattle's Capitol Hill district. Our server told us that Plum Bistro would soon be launching a crowdfunding campaign to raise money to buy a new food service truck. They would use the truck, the server explained, to provide mobile lunchtime service to the crowds of working people in various neighborhoods in Seattle.

(In case you don't know, Seattle basically launched the "street food" craze that is sweeping across America. It started in 2007, when a Seattle chef, Josh Henderson, founded his own company, Skillet Street Food, and began serving gourmet "street food"—e.g., mini-burgers with arugula, goat cheese, and bacon jam—to lunchtime crowds, out of a vintage Airstream trailer. Since then, the craze has spread to other cities.)

My wife decided she would donate $1,000 to Plum Bistro's crowdfunding campaign. In return for this $1,000 donation, as part of the campaign's tiered rewards system, we received a catered dinner party. My wife and I hosted a party for six of our business associates, and Plum Bistro sent the food to our house with servers to serve our guests. It was a wonderful evening for all of us.

I'm happy to report that Plum Bistro was able to use the donations from my wife and others to buy the food truck they needed. But look closely at the reasons why their crowdfunding campaign was a success:

❑ They had a definite goal for the campaign (buying a food truck).

❑ They had an established clientele of regular customers at

their Capitol Hill restaurant.

❑ They heavily promoted the campaign, even before it started, through word-of-mouth marketing, by having their servers tell their customers about it. Once the campaign started, they continued to promote it, through their website and email marketing.

❑ They offered a good set of tiered rewards as part of their campaign, so customers who donated would get something of value.

Tip #5: Value your fear

When I first started my business, there was another publisher in the office next door to mine who was publishing his own bi-monthly newspaper. This publisher's business soon folded because he spent too much time working on his computer and not enough time making sales calls to potential advertisers for his paper. While I believe that a lack of organization was one of the major reasons his business failed, I think that was only part of it.

This publisher happened to be married to a very wealthy spouse who was a highly paid executive at one of Seattle's most famous corporations. And while the publisher wasn't a freeloader (prior to starting his own business, he himself had been a successful executive), the fact that he had other financial resources meant that he didn't have to worry as much about the success or failure of his business. If his business failed, he would still have food on the table. Because of his shared wealth, this publisher lost an important incentive to succeed: Fear! He would come in late to the office and would leave early. I never once saw him come in and work on the weekends. On the other hand, I was single and I didn't have a lot of money to fall back on. Therefore, I had a major incentive to succeed. I worked longer hours and came into work on the weekends out of a pure need to keep eating and to pay my rent.

While it's certainly best to start a business when you have another source of steady income (e.g., support from your spouse), a little fear can be a good thing. Those who worry about the success or failure of their businesses have an advantage. They are inclined to try harder, do better, and work longer hours to ensure the survival of their businesses.

~

As my colleague and very successful publisher, Larry Coffman, would often say, that "knot in your gut" isn't necessarily a bad thing.

~

Tip #6: Hire free agents

When you start your own business, surround yourself with

other free agents so you can rent their skills when you need them. When you don't need their skills anymore, move on. Of course, this doesn't mean you should end your relationship with those free agents once they've finished the job for which you hired them. You should keep in close contact with them, in case you need their services in the future. I have certain free agents that I prefer to work with, some of whom I've worked with for decades, going back to the very beginning of my business. But always remember that any business relationship you develop with a free agent is just that, a business relationship. Business is not about making friends; it's about cultivating colleagues.

Of course, if you make friends along the way, that's a bonus. Usually, however, the relationship continues only as long as both parties are benefiting financially. The relationship ends, in most cases, when that incentive goes away. In over twenty-five years in business, I've never hired any employees, and I never plan to. I do make a policy of paying free agents generously for the services they provide. I respect the people I work with and want to keep working with them for as long as possible.

When you're looking to hire a free agent, the best person to hire is someone like yourself who is sustaining her own business. Her mindset will be closest to yours. She knows that if she doesn't give you her best work, you will move on to someone else who does. Free agents who run their own enterprises usually get the job done right the first time. If they don't, they're the ones who will stay up all night correcting their mistakes. The free agents who work with me know that I *don't* tolerate missed deadlines.

Tip #7: Delegate repetitive work

As CEO of your company, it's your responsibility to create the systems that allow your business to run smoothly and efficiently. When you reach the point where you have a series of repetitive tasks that take you away from the more important aspects of your business, it's easy and cost-effective to hire free agents to handle those tasks for you.

The types of free agents you choose to work with will depend on the nature of your business. Again, when I was publishing my newspaper, I hired free agents to handle the repetitive tasks of editing and proofreading and to input the weekly articles for my paper into my laptop computer. This freed up my time as CEO of the company to make sales calls and meet with potential advertisers.

Today, I use free agents to write, produce, record, sell, and distribute radio commercials for my clients. I use a free agent who specializes in voice-overs to narrate the radio commercials and another free agent to provide sound effects. I even used a free agent to help me in writing this book and another free agent to format it as a Kindle book.

One of the very first free agents you should hire, no matter what type of business you have, is a good accountant. Don't be tempted by those websites that allow you to prepare your tax returns over the Internet and send your forms directly to the IRS. A good tax accountant can save you a ton of money in business tax deductions. In the past twenty-five years, my accountants have saved my business far more money than I've paid out for their services.

FURTHER READING

....

Books That Will Help You Think Like an Entrepreneur

- *E-Myth Revisited* by Michael Geber
- *No Limits* by Sara Morgan
- *The Big Book of Small Business* by Tom Gegax and Phil Bolsta
- *How to Succeed as a Small Business Owner...and Still Have a Life* by Bill Collier
- *Start Your Own Business* by Rieva Lesonsky
- *Work at Home Now* by Christine Durst and Michael Haaren
- *Entrepreneurs Notebook* by Steven Gold
- *The One Page Business Plan* by Jim Horan
- *Shoestring Venture* by Steve Monas
- *Making Money from Home* by Donna Partow
- *Birthing the Elephant: Women's Go for It Guide* by Karin Abarbanel
- *The Small Business Owner's Manual* by Joe Kennedy
- *What No One Ever Tells You About Starting Your Own Business* by Jan Norman
- *The Playbook for Small Businesses* by Steve Henry
- *Engineering Your Start Up* by James A. Swanson and Michael L. Baird
- *Working for Yourself: Law & Taxes* by Stephen

Fishman

- *Starting Your Own Business* by Peter Hingston
- *Starting on a Shoestring* by Arnold Goldstein
- *Taking Your Business to the Next Level* by Frances McGuckin
- *The Entrepreneur's Information Source Book* by Susan C. Awe
- *201 Great Ideas for Your Small Business: Revised and Updated* by Jane Applegate
- *The Entrepreneur's Desk Reference* by Jane Applegate
- *Succeeding in Small Business: The 101 Toughest Problems and How to Solve Them* by Jane Applegate
- *On Your Own Terms* by Jane Applegate
- *Making Money with Your Computer at Home* by Paul Edwards
- *Best Home Businesses for People 50+* by Paul and Sarah Edwards
- *Finding Your Perfect Work (Working from Home)* by Paul and Sarah Edwards
- *Getting Business to Come to You* by Paul Edwards
- *Home Businesses You Can Buy* by Paul and Sarah Edwards
- *Working from Home* by Peter Hingston and Alistair Balfour
- *Free Agent Nation* by Daniel Pink
- *The Small Business Bible* by Steven D. Strauss
- *Secrets of Self Employment* by Paul and Sarah Edwards
- *The Entrepreneur's Desk Reference Authoritative Information* by Jane Applegate
- *The Best Home Businesses of the 21st Century* by Paul and Sarah Edwards
- *Success for Less: 100 Low Cost Businesses You Can Start Today* by Rob and Terry Adams
- *Mompreneurs* by Ellen H. Paralpiano and Patricia

Cobe

- *The Economics of Self-Employment and Entrepreneurship* by Simon C. Parker
- *Thinking Like an Entrepreneur* by Peter I. Hupalo
- *What No One Ever Tells You About Starting Your Own Business* by Jan Norman
- *101 Tips for Running a Successful Home Business* by Maxye and Lou Henry
- *The Work at Home Source Book* by Lynie Arden
- *199 Great Home Businesses* by Tom Hicks
- *The Innovators Solution* by Professor Clayton Christensen and Michael Raynor
- *The Progress Paradox* by Gregg Easterbrook

Books on Accounting

- *Small Business Accounting Simplified* by Dan Sitarz
- *Keeping the Books* by Linda Pinson
- *Small Business Taxes Made Easy* by Eva Rosenberg
- *Small Business Cash Flow* by Denise O'Berry
- *Deduct It: Lower Your Small Business Taxes* by Stephen Fishman
- *Wiley Pathways Small Business Accounting Basics* by Angie Mohr
- *Tax Savvy for Small Business* by Frederick W. Daily

Books on Marketing & Success

- *Duct Tape Marketing* by John Jantsch
- *Ultimate Small Business Marketing Guide* by James Stephenson and Courtney Thurman
- *Small Business Marketing* by Stuart Atkins MBA
- *Guerilla Marketing* by Jay Conrad Levinson
- *10 Secrets of Mobile Marketing* by Patty Rutkowski
- *Maximum Marketing, Minimum Dollars* by Kim T. Gordon
- *Good to Be Great* by Jim Collins
- *Outliers* by Malcom Gladwell
- *Satisfaction: How Every Great Company Listens to the Voice of the Customer* by Chris Davone and James D. Power
- *Public Speaking* by Stephanie Coopman and James Lull
- *Drive: The Surprising Truth About What Motivates Us* by Daniel H. Pink

ABOUT THE AUTHOR

....

Paul E. Casey is the CEO and founder of Casey Communications Inc., a full-service communications firm based in Seattle. He has hosted numerous radio shows on self-employment and has interviewed hundreds of successful entrepreneurs. After spending years working in the private and public sectors, Casey stepped into the world of self-employment. He has a Bachelor of Arts Degree in Political Science from Washington State University, is the former Chair of the Murrow Professional Advisory Board, a Trustee with the Washington State University Foundation, and part-owner of the Tacoma Rainiers of the Pacific Coast League, a AAA Affiliate of the Seattle Mariners. Casey resides in Seattle with his wife, Marti.

66088078R00117

Made in the USA
Charleston, SC
12 January 2017